FAKE STUFF

China and the Rise of Counterfeit Goods

Yi-Chieh Jessica Lin

Harvard University

Routledge
Taylor & Francis Group

NEW YORK AND LONDON

First published 2011
by Routledge
711 Third Avenue, New York, NY 10017

Simultaneously published in the UK
by Routledge
2 Park Square, Milton Park, Abingdon, Oxon OX14 4RN

Routledge is an imprint of the Taylor & Francis Group, an informa business

© 2011 Taylor & Francis

The right of Yi-Chieh Jessica Lin to be identified as author of this work has been asserted by her in accordance with sections 77 and 78 of the Copyright, Designs and Patents Act 1988.

Typeset in New Baskerville by RefineCatch Limited, Bungay, Suffolk, UK
Printed and bound in the United States of America on acid-free paper by Walsworth Publishing Company, Marceline, MO

Library of Congress Cataloging-in-Publication Data
Lin, Yi-Chieh Jessica.
Fake stuff : China and the rise of counterfeit goods / Yi-Chieh Jessica Lin.
p. cm.—(The Routledge series for creative teaching and learning in anthropology)
1. Product counterfeiting—China. 2. Consumption (Economics)—Social aspects.
3. Brand name products—Social aspects. 4. Intellectual property infringement—China. 5. China—Commerce. I. Title.
HF1040.9.C6L57 2011
364.16'680951—dc22   2010037392

ISBN 13: 978–0–415–88302–3 (hbk)
ISBN 13: 978–0–415–88303–0 (pbk)
ISBN 13: 978–0–203–82975–2 (ebk)

FAKE STUFF

The Anthropology of Stuff is part of a new series, *The Routledge Series for Creative Teaching and Learning in Anthropology*, dedicated to innovative, unconventional ways to connect undergraduate students and their lived concerns about our social world to the power of social science ideas and evidence. Our goal is to help spark social science imaginations and in doing so, new avenues for meaningful thought and action. Each "Stuff" title is a short text illuminating for students the network of people and activities that create their material world.

Yi-Chieh Jessica Lin reveals how the entrepreneurial energy of emerging markets, such as China, includes the opportunity to profit from fake stuff, that is counterfeit goods that rely on our fascination with brand names. Students will discover how the names and logos embroidered and printed on their own clothes carry their own price tag above and beyond the use value of the products themselves. The book provides a wonderful introduction for students to global markets and their role in determining how they function.

Yi-Chieh Jessica Lin holds a Ph.D. degree in Anthropology from Harvard University. She is Assistant Professor of General Education at the National Chung-Hsing University, Taiwan. She has published short stories and essays in various Chinese newspapers since 1994. She worked as a television reporter for China Television Company in the past and produced documentaries on post-earthquake reconstructions.

The Routledge Series for Creative Teaching and Learning in Anthropology
Editor: Richard H. Robbins, SUNY at Plattsburgh

This series is dedicated to innovative, unconventional ways to connect under-graduate students and their lived concerns about our social world to the power of social science ideas and evidence. Our goal is to help spark social science imaginations and in doing so, new avenues for meaningful thought and action.

Available

Re-Imagining Milk by Andrea S. Wiley
Coffee Culture by Catherine M. Tucker
Lycra by Kaori O'Connor

Forthcoming

Reading the iPod as an Anthropological Artifact by Lane DeNicola

For my family

CONTENTS

SERIES FOREWORD

The premise of these short books on the anthropology of stuff is that stuff talks, that written into the biographies of everyday items of our lives—coffee, T-shirts, computers, iPods, flowers, drugs, and so forth—are the stories that make us who we are and that makes the world the way it is. From their beginnings, each item bears the signature of the people who extracted, manufactured, picked, caught, assembled, packaged, delivered, purchased and disposed of it. And in our modern market-driven societies, our lives are dominated by the pursuit of stuff.

Examining stuff is also an excellent way to teach and learn about what is exciting and insightful about anthropological and sociological ways of knowing. Students, as with virtually all of us, can relate to stuff, while, at the same time, discovering through these books that it can provide new and fascinating ways of looking at the world.

Stuff, or commodities and things are central, of course, to all societies, to one extent or another. Whether it is yams, necklaces, horses, cattle, or shells, the acquisition, accumulation and exchange of things is central to the identities and relationships that tie people together and drive their behavior. But never, before now, has the craving for stuff reached the level it has; and never before have so many people been trying to convince each other that acquiring more stuff is what they most want to do. As a consequence, the creation, consumption, and disposal of stuff now threatens the planet itself. Yet to stop or even slow down the manufacture and accumulation of stuff would threaten the viability of our economy, on which our society is built.

This raises various questions. For example, what impact does the compulsion to acquire stuff have on our economic, social, and political well-being, as well as on our environment? How do we come to believe that there are certain things that we must have? How do we come to value some commodities or form of commodities above others? How have we managed to create commodity chains that link peasant farmers in Colombia or gold miners in Angola to wealthy residents of New York or teenagers in Nebraska? Who comes up with the ideas for stuff and how do they translate those ideas into things for people to buy? Why do we sometimes consume stuff that is not very good for us? These short books examine such questions, and more.

The story of "fake" stuff, or counterfeit goods as told by Yi-Chieh Jessica Lin reveals a fascination for so-called brand names on the one hand, and getting a bargain on the other. Names and logos carry a price tag; companies that produce common items—shoes, soft drinks, clothing, and electronics—have succeeded in attaching value to their brand and are able, as a consequence, to charge consumers considerably more than the same product without the name. This, of course, has opened the door to entrepreneurs able to produce largely the same item, with a slightly different name (e.g. i-Orange, Vike, etc.), or even the same name, as Yi-Chieh Jessica Lin relates, and sell it at a far lower price. China, now bursting with entrepreneurial energy, has taken full advantage of the opportunity offered by this market niche to become the center of the global trade in counterfeit goods. But Professor Lin also tells a larger story of the debate over intellectual property rights, the chain that links fashion designers in Paris to assembly plants in China, and, how fake stuff creates, not just the opportunity for profit, but for protest as well. After reading this book, you'll never look at fake stuff the same way again.

Richard Robbins
Series Editor

PREFACE

Do I get arrested if I accidentally carry a fake Prada bag when I go to Italy? Should I buy the knockoff cell phone when it has solar batteries and is ten times cheaper than a brand name one? Why are most of the counterfeit goods in the world made in China? As an anthropologist, I am interested in the above questions as well as the nuances of an emerged knockoff culture in China and issues of "authenticity" and "morality." This "knockoff" or *shanzhai* (literally meaning "bandit") culture is fueled by the waves of Post-Fordism and other trends in global economy, consumerism, the culture of Chinese migrant workers and the entrepreneurial spirit springing up in the tiny apartments in various cities of China.

This book is devoted to better undergraduate students' understanding of globalization, commodity flows, business ethics, intellectual property rights, and Chinese economy. While Andrew Mertha, Tim Philips, William Alford, Hillel Schwartz and many others have covered politics and the history of piracy, my book offers a critical ethnography of copy culture and consumer society from a bottom-up perspective and addresses the intersection of formal and informal economy, or the "gray zones." When I started teaching a General Education course of Copy Culture and Consumerism at National Chung-Hsing University of Taiwan in Spring 2010, I received much useful feedback from the students, whose majors range from Veterinary Science, Electrical Engineering, and Business Management to Chinese Literature. Many of them expressed their wishes to have a textbook for the course to study the topic more systematically. Yuson Jung, who taught a course of Consumer Society in Fall 2009 at Harvard University also encouraged me to publish a textbook and provided invaluable suggestions and feedback from Harvard students, some of whom read my Ph.D. dissertation for Jung's class. The book is particularly useful for courses of Globalization Studies, Chinese Society, Anthropology of Consumerism and Introduction to Anthropology.

Much of the present manuscript was written when I taught as Assistant Professor in General Education at National Chung-Hsing University in Taichung, Taiwan since 2009. Particular thanks go to Han-Sen Hung for his extremely able assistance with some of the figure drawing. I gratefully acknowledge the support of the series editor Professor Richard Robbins as well as my Ph.D. advisor, Theodore Bestor. The Anthropology Professor Michael Herzfeld at Harvard University has enthusiastically collected invaluable data in Europe and Korea. I am grateful for the constructive criticisms and help from Steve Rutter, Leah Babb-Rosenfeld, Maria Mussachio, Dung-An Wang, Xi He, May-yi Shaw, Andrea Del Bono, and Hsaio-Lung Ni. The love and patience of the above all helped the book to materialize. However, I remain solely responsible for the findings, interpretations and conclusions expressed in the book.

1

INTRODUCTION

On a hot and humid summer day in 2006, the Xiangyang Market offered up hundreds of outdoor stalls and "brand name" goodies: Louis Vuitton wallets, Gucci monogrammed handbags, and Prada key rings neatly lined rolling carts as vendors yelled loudly, "Good stuff here, you should take a look!" Only in the 2008 Beijing Olympics closing ceremony would one find a place so densely packed. Non-Chinese customers were the majority, some of them carrying large suitcases behind them to accommodate their "souvenirs." Inside those cases were bags, scarves, watches and other goods—a potpourri of local market commodities with global cache.

A young vendor named Jiaming Chen beckoned customers to inspect his goods: "Feel free to take a closer look and touch any of these wallets or bags . . . I have more in the back." Jiaming, who appeared to be in his twenties, wore jeans, a black rock 'n' roll T-shirt, and a pair of old running shoes. His hair, dyed blonde, contrasted sharply with his dark black eyebrows. "How much is this Louis Vuitton wallet?" A customer asked. "RMB 100," Jiaming replied. The customer put it back. "What about 80?" Jiaming offered. "Wait. Let me get some better stuff from the back. Don't leave." Within seconds, Jiaming disappeared into another room, reappearing with four wallets of a different style. "These are all 'double A' quality goods that I am selling at RMB 80 each," he declared.

In the end, the customer walked away. But there would be many more customers on this hot summer day. And their only shelter from the sun on this day and others would be under the shadow of two trees, between which hung a red banner with large white Chinese characters that read, "Our mission is to knock down counterfeit goods and protect intellectual property rights."

Counterfeit Culture

Xiangyang Market used to be a novelty for tourists from around the world. It was first opened in 2000 in downtown Shanghai as part of a plan by the Municipal Government to boost the city's economy. Today, relocated and renamed the Xinyang Market, it is one of many counterfeit markets in China. Counterfeit markets, of course, blossomed before China's economic liberalization, when goods were not easily accessible to China's consumers under the formal and tightly regulated economy. But in contemporary China, counterfeit markets have expanded in scope and size. Whereas authentic brand name goods are delivered to state-owned or foreign-owned stores through formal channels, counterfeit goods flow into open-air wholesale markets located in densely populated areas that can be easily accessed by public transportation.

Though they operate above ground and quite visibly, these markets occupy a kind of "gray zone" between the formal and informal economy. In these gray zones, the "fake" outstrips the real, and questions of authenticity are routinely destabilized and even made arbitrary. These grays zones and this burgeoning "fake" culture have become fodder for artists and politicians alike. In 2007, curator Pauline Yao of Universal Studios, Beijing hosted an art exhibition with counterfeiting as its theme. The exhibition, entitled "Forged Realities," featured ten young, avant-garde artists from around the world and tackled the distinction between fakery and reality, truth and fiction, fact and fantasy.[1]

In 2008, the Brooklyn Museum featured more than ninety works of Takashi Murakami, the designer who collaborated with Louis Vuitton. In the exhibit, Murakami displayed his bags for Louis Vuitton as if they were for sale on Chinatown sidewalks. The display was named "Monogramouflage" and was designed to bring attention to the rise in Louis Vuitton counterfeits.[2] And in Dafen Village, Shenzhen, China, over 8,000 painters, artisan–painters and apprentices are working to produce commissioned paintings of Western masterpieces (e.g. Van Gogh).

Fake stuff is possible, of course, only in an economy in which, for many products, their most important feature is their name. When people buy Coca-Cola, they are not buying only colored, sweetened water; they are buying a Coke and all the meaning and symbolism that have been constructed around the name. In the case of Coke, as with many other products, their value comes not from creating products, but creating consumers for specific brands. Consequently the value of the sign, that is the logos and brand images, is far greater than the material product itself, be it a soft drink, sneaker, shirt, or handbag. Thus a cell phone made with pennies in Asian factories sells for dollars of symbolism created through design, branding, and advertising (see Foster 2008: 76).

In fact, the Coca-Cola corporation considers itself a marketing company, rather than a soft drink manufacturer and historically, rigorously guarded itself from companies calling themselves Coa-Kola, Coke Ola and Koke Company of America. Their efforts resulted ultimately in a U.S. Supreme Court ruling in which Justice Oliver Wendell Holmes, writing for the majority stated that "the name [Coca-Cola] characterizes a beverage to be had at almost any soda fountain. It means a single thing coming from a single source and well known in the community" (see Foster 2008: 79).

But since the price of things may include the cost of the name, counterfeiting has become a cultural touchstone as consumers seek the symbolism of the brand, without having to pay its cost. In Mandarin Chinese, counterfeit goods are known as *jiahuo, kelong* or *fangmaopin. Jia* and *fangmao* are both expressions for "counterfeiting"; *huo* and *pin* are both expressions for "goods." *Kelong* is a transliteration of the English word "clone." Another term for counterfeit good is *shanzhai,* which literally refers to "mountain fortress" and figuratively refers to bandits in mountain hideaways taking potshots at the established giants in Robin Hood fashion. There are many categories of *shanzhai* products, ranging from food, fashion accessories, clothes, perfumes, flat tires, aircraft parts, automobiles, medicine, watches, purses, tea pots, money, MP3 players, flat-screen computers, and cellular phones to amusement parks. *Time Magazine* even produced a list of top ten Chinese knockoffs: Hi Phone and Aphone A6, iPed, Goojje, Nat Nat Shoes, Shanzhai Street, China's White Houses, China's Next Top Model, Shanghai's World Expo Song, China's Fine-Art Factory, Huanhai Landscape VA3, and Lifan 320 (Bergman 2010).

In 1949, after Chiang Kai-Shek's Kuomintang (Chinese Nationalist Party) retreated to the island of Taiwan after their defeat by the Communist Party of Mao Zedong at the conclusion of a bitter 30-year-long civil war, many former entrepreneurs of Shanghai fled to Hong Kong, where they started new businesses. Local imitations of these newcomers' crafts appeared in the late 1940s and 1950s. *Shanzhai* referred to these local imitations, which involved three to five workers from the same family who composed unauthorized products to sell. Gradually, the term evolved to refer to homemade and counterfeit products. In January of 2009, Google published its annual rankings of China's new hotwords. *Shanzhai* ranked the first.[3]

Some studies suggest that the prevalence of counterfeiting in China can be attributed to a cultural tradition that emphasizes memorizing literature word by word in traditional education. Others traced back the emphasis of good forgery as a criterion for good calligraphy to the Sixth Dynasty. Ultimately, however, much of the counterfeiting can be attributed to China's emergence in the past thirty years as a world economic power. In 2010, China became the second largest economy in the world, after the United States. After the victory of the communists over the nationalists in 1949, China instituted a Marxist, state-run economy. But after various economic and social upheavals, in 1992, Premier Deng Xiaoping advocated for a total market economy during his itinerary to southern China and accelerated the economic growth. Overall, the Economic Reform has helped reduce the poverty rate from 53 percent of the population in the Mao Zedong era to 19 percent in 1985, and 6 percent in 2001. But there are still significant differences in income between city and rural dwellers. According to the official statistics, the average annual income for a Chinese peasant in 2009 was $754, 41 percent of which is spent on food. The average annual income for an urban resident is higher: $2,514 with 36.5 percent of the income spent on food.

The switch to a more market-oriented economy unleashed enormous entrepreneurial energy, some of it directed toward producing counterfeit goods. Still, I focus on the production of counterfeiting in China because China's counterfeiting operations are central to global debates over intellectual property rights. China is not the only place of counterfeiting production. My friend Kedron Thomas, a Ph.D. candidate in Anthropology at Harvard University, has conducted more than one year of fieldwork on counterfeiting in Guatemala. My other friends based in U.S. academic institutions have also engaged in research on counterfeiting in Brazil, India, Cote d'Ivoire, Indonesia, Macedonia, Turkey, Vietnam, and Romania. But China's export might be the largest among them. I hope by focusing on the cases of Chinese production counterfeiting, we focus attention on the issue of business ethics and globalization. In other words, wars of intellectual property rights need to be understood in the context of corporate social responsibility, consumerism and the global economy.[4]

Intellectual Property Rights

China's counterfeiting operations are central to global debates over intellectual property rights. The World Trade Organization (WTO) defines intellectual property rights as "rights given to people over the creation of their minds. Creators can be given the right to prevent others from using their inventions, designs or other creations."[5] This definition implies that an intellectual property right is an exclusive right, and this exclusive right is given by the state according to state law. Exclusivity grants that the holder of an intellectual property right can forbid other people from using the intellectual property.[6] Any exploitation of the intellectual property rights without the owner's permission constitutes infringement. The law does not require the owner to practice his or her intellectual property rights in order to keep them. Thus, to fully understand intellectual property rights, that is, how people can own ideas or symbols, we need to know a little about copyright law.

Intellectual property rights are often secured through a trademark. Trademarks, which consist of words, shapes, marks, colors, sounds, or some combination thereof, function as symbols of a certain brand. In China, Taiwan or the United States, once a trademark application is approved for registration in the trademark office, it is valid for a period of ten years. In the modern regime of intellectual property rights protection, two other rights—copyrights and patents—are equally valued by corporations.

Patents and copyrights secure profits for corporations, who invest in the research and development necessary to create new works and inventions.

Although these rights are often conflated, there are distinctions. Trademarks, unlike copyright and patent protection, have no constitutional basis; rather they emerged in Anglo-American jurisprudence through common law and are now protected statutorily (Alford 1995: 2). Trademarks are also more popularly recognized as brand name commodities that carry the weight of religious symbolism.[7]

In a knowledge-based economy, in which value is placed less on tangible goods and more on the creative invention of ideas and designs, the infringement of intellectual property rights has become a global economic concern. In the case of copyright piracy, there is not necessarily any attempt to convince the consumer that the pirated product was produced and distributed by the original copyright owner. Rather, most counterfeit products are identical to the genuine product and will often bear the registered or unregistered trademark of another party and the company name. In some cases, the circulation and consumption of counterfeit goods poses a serious public safety problem, as in the fake pharmaceutical drugs sold worldwide.[8]

Though counterfeiting raises a host of concerns about world trade, intellectual property, and public safety, this book tackles counterfeiting as a cultural phenomenon. It asks how counterfeit goods mediate the meaning and value we place on commodities and consumption. That is, whereas globalization has often been debated in terms of the spread of a "3M" culture—McDonald's, MTV, and Macintosh—it has also involved the spread of transnational goods and ideas that are not identified by a single origin (Watson 1997: 11). In this transnational world, what is fake and what is real? Who are the creators and who are the imitators? Where does "intellectual property" begin and where does it end? What is "genuine" stuff?

In my discussion of counterfeiting throughout this book, I define counterfeit products in three ways:

(1) Unauthorized use of a brand name or trademark (e.g. a leather bag with the letters L and V printed on it in a way that exactly replicates the Louis Vuitton logo, but without authorization from Louis Vuitton);
(2) Intentional resemblance of a brand name product (e.g. a pair of running shoes that are designed to look like a pair of Nike shoes, but have the name Vike and a checkmark rather than a swoosh);
(3) Unauthorized sale of unauthorized production or overstock (e.g. a pair of Nike running shoes or a Louis Vuitton leather bag, the sale of which is not authorized).

The fact that there is a range, or continuum of these practices suggests that there is also a range of social meanings that applies to these goods and that drives the market for their sale and purchase.

The Meaning of Counterfeit Goods

A study of contemporary counterfeit goods sheds light on how values are negotiated in different cultural settings in people's daily life.[9] As Arjun Appadurai and Igor Kopytoff (1986) suggest, value is sought after or externalized in things. When Marx reflected on what he called the fetishism of commodities, he suggested that we look at the social forms that commodities embody. In contrast to the classical economist's emphasis on market supply and demand, Marx emphasized the social form of labor and the exchange value that the commodity possesses. He pointed out that the mystical character of the commodity does not come from how it is used (its use value) but from the labor of private individuals. In later studies of consumption, anthropologists saw the social form of the commodity being elaborated through three kinds of values people seek in consumption— exchange value (how the commodity can be used to exchange for something else), use value and identity value, or what the commodity says about the person owning it. Identity value is associated with consumption (Warde 1997: 59). Advertising in the present day creates and attaches identity value to certain commodities. It is also sometimes termed "added value," as in Martin Davidson's work.

Martin Davidson, in his book *The Consumerist Manifesto* also refers to identity value as "added value." Brands, he says, are "products with something extra" (Davidson 1992: 23). Through consuming the added values of brand-name products, people are also able to mark a distinction between "the taste of luxury (of freedom) and the tastes of necessity" (Bourdieu 1984: 177). When one consumes a brand name product, he or she is not only consuming the use value of the product itself but also its added value, such as a sense of being elegant and sophisticated. When someone drinks Coca-Cola, the product is associated with all the images created in advertisements—the music, and the mood—and which then attaches to the consumer. The social aspect of consuming brand name products can be easily identified by the showiness of brand logos—they are social symbols that mark one's economic and social status. The nature of contemporary shopping (or consumption) is, according to Daniel Miller (1998: ix), "a social process that goes well beyond the isolating act of purchase into cycles of use and re-use as the meaning of goods is transformed through their incorporation into people's daily life." But how do counterfeit goods fit into our understanding of consumption and the values we attach to it?

Counterfeit products are not just imitations of Western brand names. They reflect broader cultural politics expressed through consumer goods. However, individuals from different cultural backgrounds and locales have different perceptions of and attach different meanings to counterfeit goods, and those meanings deviate greatly from the meanings what were attached to the brand name originals.

Although money-making is a major force propelling this industry, in China, the industry is also driven by the desire to create a shared sense of cultural intimacy, at both regional and national levels. As we will see in later chapters of the book, the copy culture emerged as a way for consumers to resist and reclaim control of meanings from a changing economic system.

The scope of the counterfeit market is no small matter. Economists estimate that the size of the American underground economy is over US$1 trillion, or close to 10 percent of the GDP of the United States. According to the International Anti-Counterfeiting Coalition, counterfeiting has cost U.S. businesses between US$200 billion and US$250 billion annually.[10] Trade in counterfeit merchandise is responsible for the loss of more than 750,000 American jobs a year (International Anti-Counterfeiting Coalition 2010). America's biggest firms spend US$2–4 million annually to combat counterfeiting (Economist 2010).

The European media report that the number of counterfeit products seized by French customs totaled 3.5 million items in 2004 alone. This figure includes 9,000 square meters of cloth bearing the label of luxury accessories

Table 1.1 **Fakes by the Numbers**

$600 Billion The estimated annual sales in counterfeit products worldwide
$200 Billion The minimum estimated loss to American companies from counterfeit products
$27 Billion The estimated annual sales in counterfeit products in USA in 2008
$1 Billion The minimum estimated annual loss in tax revenues in New York City due to counterfeiting
$272 Million The estimated domestic value of all counterfeit products seized by U.S. customs in 2008
75 000 Number of American jobs lost due to the counterfeit goods trade
36% The percentage of Chinese footwear in all IPR infringing cases in 2008
$1.69 The average amount paid by Chinatown wholesalers to import a fake blank watch
7% The estimated percentage of world trade represented by counterfeit goods

Source: Adapted from International Anti-Counterfeiting Coalition website, the *Economist*, and other news reports

manufacturer Louis Vuitton, 542,000 false prescription medicines, and 480,000 fake watch batteries just to name a few. It is estimated that the counterfeit business has resulted in 100,000 lost jobs in Europe, and revenue losses for "real" brand name companies are as high as 250 billion Euros.[11]

On a global scale, trade in counterfeit goods has been one of the fastest growing industries. While visiting China in 2004, United States Assistant Secretary of Commerce William Lash pointed out that the trade in counterfeit merchandise accounted for roughly 7 percent of global commerce and each year cost legitimate companies worldwide about US$50 billion (Simons 2005: 1). Furthermore, since 1982, trade in illegitimate goods has increased from $5.5 billion to approximately $600 billion annually, accounting for approximately 5 to 7 percent of total world trade.

Methodology and Fieldwork

Studying counterfeit markets poses methodological challenges. Because counterfeiting is "underground," no reliable statistics exist to measure and assess its meaning for consumers worldwide. In addition, the meaning we attach to things is a subjective matter not easily captured in quantitative data. In the absence of statistical data and meaningful quantitative measures, qualitative research methods become crucial in probing this social phenomenon. Thus, the data for this book comes from qualitative field work that I conducted between 2004 and 2008. From 2004 to 2006, I visited mainland China at least once a year to visit different markets. Preliminary archival research on newspapers and reports on counterfeiting problems in China revealed that Xiangyang Market (Shanghai), Xiushui Market (Beijing), and LuoHu Mall (Shenzhen) have been the most important retail markets for "knockoffs." Of these markets, I focused on those in Shanghai and Shenzhen.

There are at least five major wholesale counterfeit markets in China and they supply the entire coastal region and major cities of China: Hanzhen Jie (Wuhan City, Hubei Province); Linyi Market (Linyi, Shandong Province); Nansantiao Market (Shijiazhuang, Hebei Province); China Small Commodities City (Yiwu City, Zhejiang Province); and Wuai Market (Shenyang, Liaoning Province).[12] Among the major wholesale markets I chose one—Yiwu—to study. The research sites included Taiwan and New York City because the former had been a transferring port for international counterfeit trade and the latter features a high share of counterfeit merchandise (8 percent of all counterfeit merchandise in the United States).[13]

In addition to studying these markets, I worked for eleven months at a transnational furniture supplier to Wal-Mart and Home Depot. The supplier, Chinan Co. Ltd., has operated several factories in Dongguan in the Pearl River Delta since the 1990s. The Taiwanese company moved its production base to China in

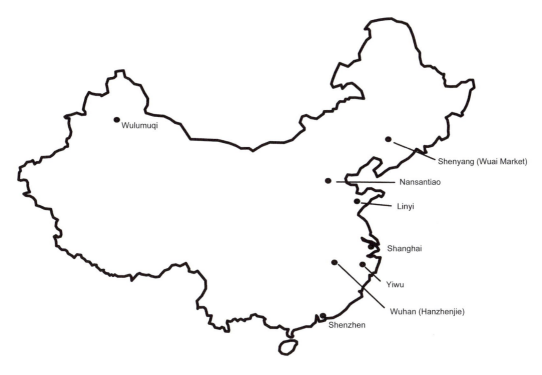

Figure 1.1 **Map of Major Wholesale Markets in China.**

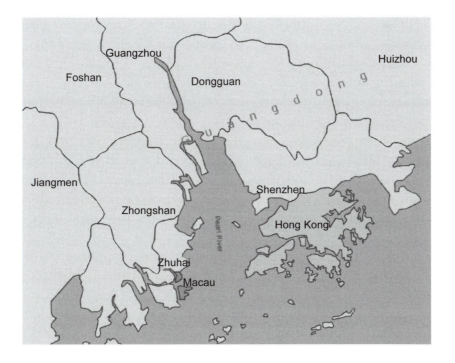

Figure 1.2 **Map of Pearl River Delta.**

the 1990s in order to save on labor costs, and successfully acquired orders from Wal-Mart and Home Depot. It quickly grew to the largest supplier in the world of the specific kind of furniture that it produces. Using employees of Chinan as an entrée, I was able to interview sellers and consumers of copycat cell phones, bootlegged purses and other counterfeit products in Shenzhen.

The bulk of China's workforce is made up of young, rural women who have become the backbone of the country's industrial expansion. The culture that these women and their Taiwanese managers helped construct fueled a vibrant copycat culture in the streets outside the factory gates.

In 2010, the average monthly salary of an operator in Chinan Co. Ltd. ranged from RMB 1,200–1600, or US$175–234. An operator in an electronics company earned an average of US$200 per month. The operators receive free meals and free housing in a dormitory annexed to the factory. The management team's dormitory, where I stayed, was in the same building. Dormitory rooms, even for managers, were quite small. My room, which was typical, was about 18 square meters with private bathroom. My neighbor at the time, a vice manager in the finance department, shared this same size space with his wife and four-year-old son.

A shared entertainment room was across the hallway, where staff watched Chinese and foreign channels on satellite television and played ping-pong after the final shift at 9 pm. Grocery stores and cheap restaurants with cuisines from various provinces were scattered around the streets between factories. Staff were not allowed to step outside the factory during non-working hours since armed robberies were common on the boulevards and in the supermarkets. However, the staff shared a company vehicle to travel to massage salons and karaoke bars for entertainment. Others frequented hostess clubs, purchased pirated copies of movies, or shopped for fake brand-name merchandise in downtown Dongguan or Shenzhen.

This production culture served as the backdrop to the burgeoning counterfeit culture in Shenzhen. Outside the factory, I conducted interviews with sellers, consumers, fashion magazine editors, clothing fashion designers, police officers, lawyers specializing in intellectual property rights, government officials, scholars and librarians in Tokyo, Taipei, Taichung, and in Boston and New York City.

The purpose of the book is to represent the diversity and nuances of China's contemporary counterfeit culture. The main focus is China, but I will incorporate cases from other countries and regions as well. In Chapter 2, I lay out the production process in the "fake" industry and tackle the network behind the production. Chapter 3 covers the distribution of fake goods. Chapter 4 deals with the meanings and risks of consuming counterfeit. In Chapter 5, I will come back to the issue of empowerment and culture jamming against consumerism.

Class Exercise

1. What are the three major types of intellectual property rights? Before and during modern times, has China regulated protection of intellectual property rights? How? When and where did the first counterfeiting take place in human history?

2

THE STRUCTURE OF A COUNTERFEIT INDUSTRY

China as the World's Factory

Yiwei Tsai went to Shenzhen City, Guangdong Province to find a job in 2003. She had just graduated from junior high school and was incredibly homesick and eager to contact family on a regular basis. A cell phone would have eased much of her loneliness, but she could not afford one. In her mind, cell phones were a luxury that her 1,000 RMB (US$146) monthly salary could ill afford. By 2007, Yiwei was working in a cell phone workshop, which afforded her the opportunity to own her own cell phone. Only it did not afford her enough time to use it. During the busiest months, she would log between 200 and 300 hours per month overtime. Even during slow months, she worked a 9–6, Sunday to Saturday work week.

The work hours and work pace in Yiwei's cell workshop were not unusual. But her cell workshop was unusual in at least one respect: the cell phones made there were not brand name cell phones; they were counterfeits. Nicknamed *shanzhai* cell phones, or copycat cell phones by competitors and customers alike, the cell phones on which Yiwei worked were functional, often fancy, but wholeheartedly fake, that is, imitations of popular foreign brands which were actually manufactured in China. Cell phone workshops like Yiwei's made huge profits, in part due to the large number of migrant workers in China who preferred a cheap cell phone to an imported brand name cell phone.

Before the *shanzhai* cell phone, there was the *shanzhai* car. First released in China in the early 2000s, the popular QQ model was developed by Chinese carmaker Chery as an imitation of General Motor's *Chevrolet*. The production of *shanzhai* cell phones and cars intermingle with the production of authentic products in the booming export industries of Shenzhen and Dongguan in the Pearl River Delta of southern China. Here, 11 million employees work in factories to supply a dizzying variety of commodities for the domestic and international market. The value of goods exported to other countries reached 405 billion RMB (US$59.8 billion), constituting 64 percent of total industrial output in China in 2007. Since the mid-1990s, Shenzhen City has focused on the development of seven major export industries including computer software, information technology, microelectronics and components, video and audio products, electro-mechanical integration, and products in the light and energy industries. These industries alone are responsible for 76 percent of Shenzhen's phenomenal economic growth, and new industries keep emerging, such as pharmaceuticals, medical equipment, and biotechnology.

The backbone of Shenzhen's economy is workers like Yiwei, who after six years in the city moved from being a production line worker to a cell phone sales representative. Having first thought of cell phones as luxury items, she had come to see them as toys, telling me, "[Cell phones] are no high technology, and any normal person should be able to make them." She uses a Nokia 6300 model cell phone with no Nokia trademark. "It is a fake . . .," she explained. "If you offer me 300RMB (US$49), it's yours." For foreign tourists who visit her store, Yiwei has advertisements in English, Chinese, Vietnamese, Indonesian, Arabic, and Hindu. And her *shanzhai* cell phones compete with new brand names like "Song Ericsson," "Nokir," and "Sanxin"—imitations of famous cell phone brands "Sony Ericsson," "Nokia" and "Samsung." In Seg Electronics market, where most of these phones are marketed, I found imitations of i-Phones called "HIPONE," "PHONE," even "i-Orange," replete with a citrusy logo, to mimic Apple.

Figure 2.1 **Seg Market (Front).**

Figure 2.2 **Seg Market (Inside).**

Some of the cell phones have a Bird's Nest Stadium or a Beijing Olympics torch emblazoned on the handset. Others employed the designs of famous sports cars. They all had the standard features of brand name cell phones: cameras, MP3, MP4, touch-screen, Bluetooth, and memory disk. Whereas a brand name cell phone might cost 4,000RMB ($585), a copy might cost just 430RMB ($63).

The prices for *shanzhai* cell phones were low, but profits high. Yiwei's boss cut down on production costs by not paying value-add taxes imposed on cell phone makers like Nokia and Sony Ericsson. He did not have to pay to submit his cell phones for standard product testing by Center Testing International, which cost brand name manufacturers upwards of around US$35,000. Nor did he pay for advertisements on television or in public spaces. And of course, he never paid the US$500,000 to research and develop the product, since he simply copied existing brand name cell phone models. Thus, after investing 4 million RMB in start-up costs for a *shanzhai* cell workshop, a manufacturer like Yiwei's boss might realize a 50–100 RMB profit per phone. Manufacturers take about 10 percent of the profit margin, distributors an additional 10–25 percent, and retailers the remaining 65–80 percent. Since retailers make a higher profit selling the *shanzhai* cell phones, they are more popular than brand name cell phones among the retailers themselves. Given these figures, and the popularity of cheap cell phones among Shenzhen's workers, thousands of *shanzhai* workshops have cropped up throughout the city.

Figure 2.3 **Fake Porsche Cell Phone (Front).**

Figure 2.4 **Fake Porsche Cell Phone (Back).**

Shijie Xia studied industrial design and ran a design studio in Shanghai. In a chic Japanese restaurant, he took out a stylish, top-of-the-line cell phone and explained: "The start-up costs for counterfeiting cell phones is low. A counterfeiter only needs to laser scan a real cell phone like this to get data on size measurements. With the information, a counterfeit cell phone can be made

Table 2.1 **A Cost Analysis of Fake Cell Phones**

Cost Structure		Brand Name Cell Phone: Vertical Equipment Production	Shanzhai Cell Phone: "Specialization Production"
Cell Phone Design	Hardware	• Research and Development Expenses • Patent Loyalties	• "Turn-Key" Solutions, or Low-Quality Components
	Software	• Research and Development Expenses • Patent Loyalties	
Cell Phone Production		• Professional OEM Factory Production • Quality Control • Official Examination	• Family Workshop or Small Factory Production • Quality Control Not Available • Official Examination Not Available
Distribution		• Middle- and Large-size Distribution • Customer Services (Repair, Replacement and Return)	• Region-Based Network of Distribution • Customer Services Not Available
Brand Management		• Global Marketing, Advertising and Brand Management	• No Advertising • No Brand Management • Counterfeiting Logo or Intentional Resemblance
Sales		• Paying Operation Taxes • Through Retail Electronics Stores	• Avoiding Operation Taxes • Sales Through Retail Electronics Stores

with ready-made software over night, thanks to the development of three dimensional drawing technologies on the computer and other computer technologies." Cell phone counterfeiting mushroomed after a Taiwanese cell phone chip designer called MediaTek developed and marketed low price, multifunction cell phone chips to Chinese cell phone workshops beginning in 2006.[1] After that time, anyone could start a production line of cell phones by assembling three components: a MediaTek chip, a cell phone case, and batteries. The workshop owners can purchase tooling, screen, earphones, batteries, chargers, and cameras manufactured locally and assemble these components together to sell in the markets. Thus, MediaTek's chairman, Ming-Kai Tsai, has been described in the Chinese newspaper *Southern Weekend* as the "Godfather" of the *shanzhai* cell phone industry. Among foreign cell phone makers, of course, he is less revered, having made possible the easy replication of brand name cell phones. This replication was made all the more easy in 2007, when the China General Office of the State Council annulled cell phone production regulations that had been on the books. This action legalized and further promoted the production of *shanzhai* cell phones.

"Lifestyling" Fake Cell Phones

Shanzhai products reflect the taste and needs of their consumers. *Shanzhai* cell phones gained popularity because they are locally-produced products that speak to Chinese customers' needs and desires, as opposed to the top-down development and marketing models of European- and American-owned cell phone companies. One *shanzhai* cell phone workshop came up with a model that featured seven speakers so that Chinese farmers could leave the phones on the perimeter of their fields and still hear them. Another *shanzhai* cell phone is equipped with four light-emitting diode (LED) lights for marketing to rural areas of China, where people still need to use cell phones as flashlights. There is also a "senior *shanzhai* cell phone," which features an enlarged screen, an enlarged keyboard, a one-click radio function and a battery standby time of 15 days.

Shanzhai cell phones constituted some 30 percent of the Chinese cell phone market in 2008. Market analysts estimate that the annual sales of *shanzhai* cell phones reached US$73.2 billion in 2009. Beijing Tianyu Communication Equipment Co. Ltd (also known as K-Touch), a cell phone maker founded in 2002, recently became the most successful cell phone maker in China next to Nokia, Samsung and Motorola. The founder and president of Tianyu, Xiuli Rong, is known as the "Godmother" of *shanzhai* cell phones because Tianyu was among the first companies to adopt the MediaTek chip and to complete the cycle from design to mass manufacture in just three months. Tianyu does not have its own sales department, but franchises retailers in the cities. The retailers pay advances to Tianyu and Tianyu ships the goods to them. Tianyu has ambitions to expand exports to overseas markets, in particular Southeast Asia and the Middle East, where demand for cheap cell phones is high. In 2007, 4.76 million Tianyu cell phones were exported to these regions.

How have brand name manufacturers responded to the rise in *shanzhai* cell phone companies? Samsung offered to collaborate and cooperate with a *shanzhai* workshop, but the workshop turned them down. Samsung had manufactured the "next generation" touch screen cell phone called "Anycall" OMNIA (SGH-i900). The *shanzhai* version is named "Anycat" and sells for one-fifth of the price of an "Anycall." Samsung had investigated the "Anycat" and found, to its astonishment, that the pirated version was not inferior to the real one. When they offered to collaborate with the *shanzhai* "Anycat" workshop, the workshop refused because they could avoid taxes and testing by remaining independent.

Yengong Lu, CEO of Lenovo Mobile in China, publicly admitted that *shanzhai* cell phones affected their market shares. Competition from *shanzhai* cell phones reduced the profit for each Lenovo product from 30 to 10 percent. The competition from *shanzhai* cell phones has also pushed down prices for cell phones in the market in general. The market price for cell phones has dropped from 1,000–1,500 RMB in 2003 to 500–1,000 RMB in 2007.

The *shanzhai* cell phone industry has moved from simply copying brand name cell phone models to designing new cell phone models. China Electronics Corp. acquired the Philips Electronics Research and Development Center in 2007 and made Shenzhen the center of China's cell phone design industry. Other large design houses in Shenzhen include Shenzhen Ginwave Technologies Ltd, CK Telecom Ltd and Shenzhen Top Wise Technology Co. Ltd. Shenzhen also has more than 100 mid-size companies and some small design houses that merely copy design solutions. These design houses have offices and facilities at the Shenzhen High-Tech Industrial Park and Tian'an Cyber Plaza, where some are developing their own chip platforms.

In fact, *shanzhai* products have expanded from cell phones to other consumer electronics, such as digital cameras and flat screen televisions. According to the Chinese Commerce Association of Electronics, 83 percent of Chinese families planned to purchase flatscreen televisions in 2009. In a shop in Beibaohua Building, for example, Miao Zhang sells her own brands of digital cameras and camcorders. She manufactures some 60 models with prices ranging from RMB 100–1,000. She has duplicated the *shanzhai* cell phone business model by copying well-established, popular products and adding a sticker that reads "SCNY," an imitation of the Japanese electronic products maker Sony. One of Zhang's customers said that only 1 percent of the cameras sold in Zhang's shop required repair. One 12 megapixel camera model at Zhang's shop sells for RMB 550, less than half the price of the same model manufactured by Sony.

Zhang also uses a laptop in her shop to reach customers from other provinces and countries. Her daily routine includes checking and replying to emails, as well as making phone calls to take orders and ship out merchandise. The sales executives of Sony in China claimed that they did not feel threatened by *shanzhai* cameras because of the technological complexity required to manufacture cameras. Likewise, manufacturers of flat screen televisions do not believe that *shanzhai* televisions will be competitive in terms of quality control because *shanzhai* companies use smuggled or recycled materials.

Though brand name manufacturers dismiss *shanzhai* televisions and cameras, consumers have shown keen interest (Yan 2008). One hundred kilometers away from Zhang's shop in Central Shenzhen, in Dashatou second-hand electronic market, *shanzhai* 32-inch flat screen televisions sell as low as RMB 2,750 (about $400). One seller, Ping Shao, can sell 200 to 300 flat screen televisions per month to hotels, motels, and karaoke bars. Shao was optimistic about his business prospects, largely because MediaTek had developed a cheap multifunction flat screen television chip. MediaTek also had developed multifunctional chips for digital cameras. These chips made it easy for low-end *shanzhai* manufacturers to produce flat-screen televisions and digital cameras at relatively low production costs. Taiwanese Chimei Electronics Company provided technology for CRT manufacturers in Shenzhen to convert to LCD manufacturing, which greatly improved the quality and manufacture time of *shanzhai* products.[2]

Jonney Shih, Chairman of the computer manufacturer ASUS, said that his company is planning to market its computer products to the growing *shanzhai* markets in India and China as a strategic response to the global financial crisis. He argues that it is critical to look at *shanzhai* businesses strategically and to look at the markets in India and China as a whole. In India, where 86 percent of the country's 1.15 billion people live on less than US$2.50 per day, the use of *shanzhai* products is encouraged by the government. Higher Education Secretary R. P. Agrawal announced a plan to make available the US$10 laptop in the southern city of Tiruptai in the hopes of improving the skills of millions of students. The government has earmarked more than 46 billion rupees (US$939 million) to develop a low-power laptop that works in rural areas with unreliable power supplies and poor Internet connectivity. The planned laptop is part of a push to increase the number of students in higher education and give them the technological skills needed to further boost India's economic growth.[3]

India has also encouraged the development of a low-priced car industry. Indian carmaker Tata Motors Ltd. began selling Nano, the world's cheapest car at 135,151 rupees (US$2,600), which is almost half the price of the next-cheapest model in the country. The company also plans to sell the Nano in Europe for 5,000 Euro (US$6,347) (Nair 2009). Ford Motor Company, Volkswagen Company, Hyundai, and Suzuki all plan to follow suit (Choudhury 2009). Indeed, German industry specialists predict that vehicles costing less than US$10,000 will dominate the global market and reach sales of 10 million per year worldwide.

Outside China, how do counterfeit goods achieve their success? Ademira, who exported *shanzhai* cell phones to Latin America, told me that the goods gained popularity in America because they are locally produced products that speak to lower-income customers' needs and desires, as opposed to the top-down development and marketing models of European- and American-owned cell phone companies. One *shanzhai* cell phone uses an ultimate size of battery and has a standby time of one year. Another cell phone model has attached a solar panel so that batteries can be recharged anywhere near light automatically. Another model of *shanzhai* cell phone has a detector function for fake currency notes. Although Ferrari, the Italian carmaker, has never released any cell phone model, *shanzhai* makers released a "Ferrari" cell phone model at $100. When President Barack Obama won the 44th U.S. Presidential Election in 2008, Chinese *shanzhai* merchants marketed an "Obama" cell phone model in Kenya at the same time. On the back of the cell phone, "Obama" was engraved on the top and "Yes We Can!" was underneath, targeting President Obama's supporters and fans in Africa. To match the purchasing power of Africa, the cell phone is sold at $30 with radio and flashlight functions. The merchant sold about 1,000 Obama phones in a week.

The Apartment Entrepreneurship

Besides the support of MediaTek and certain OEM companies, Shenzhen's copycat entrepreneurship has sprung up in various old apartments. According to official statistics, in 2009, high-end and innovative consumer electronics have produced an equivalent value of $117 billion of goods, which is about 90 percent of total production at a growth rate of 12 percent, compared to 2008. Cell phones made in Shenzhen accounted for 30 percent of the total market share in the world. In 2009 alone, Shenzhen made 400 million cell phones. In the backstreets, there are 3,000 design houses for copycat cell phones in apartments. These design houses used to build copycat cell phones, but now they have shifted to do IC design, software platform interface, or content and applications development.

When iPad was released on April 3, 2010 in the United States, these apartment entrepreneurs put up all nighters for iPad. In an apartment located in the backstreets of Shenzhen, 26-year-old Wang runs a copycat studio. He hired 20 engineers to design for the "pseudo-iPad." It is estimated that Shenzhen sold 1 million pseudo-iPads in 2010. In college, Wang set up website for corporations and saved his start-up fund for his fake iPhone workshop. But Wang's profit margin went down to $2 per cell phone. Wang came up with a solution. The pseudo-iPad combines the idea of an eBook reader, MP4, and Netbook. IC-chip companies, content providers, and system providers can supply new add-value applications with this new platform. A new supply chain and innovative ideas are burgeoning, inspired by the iPad model.

An engineer in the designer studio said: "We could cook when we get hungry and take a nap in the apartment." The Shenzhen Municipal Government have provided subsidies for entrepreneurs in terms of land, rent tax, and housing mortgage, and further promotes the brands for the 2,000 *shanzhai* entrepreneurs. They overall comprise of 80 percent of Chinese cell phone production.

In 2009, Shenzhen exported a total of 200 million cell phones, which are worth $13.3 billion. In India, 30 percent of cell phones in the market were Chinese *shanzhai* phones. However, those phones often lack international mobile equipment numbers. The IMEI (International Mobile Equipment Identity) is a unique 15 or 17 digit number given to every single cell phone used to identify an individual cell station to a GSM or UMTS network. The code is stored in the chip, and the number is typically found behind the battery. Each time a call is made, the telecommunications company uses the IMEI to identify the caller via a universal registry of phones. If a phone lacks an IMEI, the telecommunications company can still route the number to the destination, but it does not know which phone is making the call. The Pakistan government banned sales of IMEI-less cell phones in July 2008. The Department of Telecommunications in India's Ministry of Communications and Information Technology worries that these anonymous phones can be used by terrorists. In Madrid, Spain on December 6, 2009, police arrested eight people and confiscated IMEI-less cell phones. In another action on December 10, 2009, 100 police personnel confiscated 3,500 IMEI-less cell phones and arrested 32 sales representatives: some of the representatives were Chinese. Around the same time, the Singaporean and Korean police also arrested tens of people who purchased IMEI-less, *shanzhai* cell phones. The government of Egypt has also unveiled a plan to block all IMEI-less cell phones. Since October 2009, the GSM Association has implemented punitive charges for Chinese applications for IMEI. In the past, IMEI application has been free. Now each cell phone model was required to have a matching IMEI application, which cost $2,000. This became a serious burden for Chinese apartment entrepreneurs, who were forced to build alliances with local businesses in the import countries.

The Future of the *Shanzhai* Economy

It is difficult to predict the future of the *shanzhai* economy. At present, not even the "pirates" are immune to *shanzhai* culture; there are even *shanzhai* rip-offs of successful *shanzhai* brands, that is fakes of fakes. Some manufacturers simply put whatever fake brand name is currently hot on whatever phones they produce. The hipster designation of being *shanzhai* helps sell the phones. As Chaojun Xiao, Vice General Manager of Tianyu, explains, "We are popular among the fans of *shanzhai*. They admire our spirit, the *shanzhai* spirit" (Epstein 2009). Of course, there are criticisms of *shanzhai* cell phones and other counterfeit goods: poor processing, no customer service, and violations of intellectual property rights. And there have been scandals, such as consumer deaths from fake battery explosions. Above all, there has been the negative impact on China's reputation, with *shanzhai* culture marring China's entry into the World Trade Organization in 2001. But there have also been efforts to legitimize *shanzhai* manufacturing. In 2009, in the Fuyuan Hotel in Shenzhen, the first *shanzhai* conference was held among *shanzhai* manufacturers and suppliers. Manufacturers competed in product outlook, price, and stability and asserted that *shanzhai* was different from "fake."

The Chinese government's attitude toward *shanzhai* remains ambivalent. Kaiyuan Tao, Chief of Intellectual Property Bureau of Guangdong Province, has accused *shanzhai* of stealing from other enterprises and of violating intel-lectual property rights. In 2009, Ping Ni, as a commissar of the Chinese People's Political Consultative Conference, urged the banning of *shanzhai* production. On the other hand, some government officials see *shanzhai* production as an opportunity to innovate. "Should our government guide the popular *shanzhai* products to legalize and innovate *shanzhai*," one official said, "it would support the goal of turning Shenzhen into the global manufacture base of elec-tronics and information technology industries." Others Chinese government officials see *shanzhai* as a product of democracy and popular culture, and thus support it.

In spite of the debate over the legitimacy of counterfeit goods in China, there is the additional problem of copying that occurs in the formal economy. In other words, when is copying products from other manufacturers illegal and when is it innovation? In today's fashion industry, the brand name Zara has taken the lead in fast-fashion and its secret to success is that it moves faster than other brands and supplies at a cheaper price. With an in-house design team based in La Coruña, Spain, the company maintains a tightly controlled factory and distribution network and takes its designs from drawing board to store shelf in two weeks. Zara is often criticized because its designers mix and match the ideas of top fashion designers and mass produce them all over the world. Zara consumers, of course, care less about the copyright than how the design looks. Regardless, the core competitive power of the company is its ability to copy and modify, which is shared by the *shanzhai* economy in China.

The failure rate of new products by Zara is only 1 percent, compared with an average of 10 percent for the garment sector. The company only produces batches of clothing in small quantities and when the design is not popular with customers, Zara's store owners ship them to the distribution center to be sold at other locations or close-out stores. Thus, it can cut its losses quickly and move on to another trend. Several dozen items are designed each day, accumulated to actual production of 11,000 items a year, including several hundred thou-sand SKUs given variation in color, fabric, and sizes. New products are shipped to the stores twice a week. The major competitors produce on average 2,000–4,000 items a year.

Close to nine months before the start of a season, Zara's designers attend trade fairs and ready-to-wear fashion shows in Paris, New York, London, and Milan, refer to catalogs of luxury brand collections, and then develop the initial sketches of its own collection. The rapid turnover rate of merchandise creates a sense of anxiety: "Buy now because you won't see the item later." Unlike other competitors, Zara carefully protects itself from creating too strong a presence for the brand or an image of the "Zara Woman" or the "Zara Girl." Zara spends only 0.3 percent of its revenue on media advertising, compared with 3–4 percent for most specialty retailers. The freshness of its offerings, the creation of a sense of scarcity, an attractive ambience around them, and the positive word-of-mouth resulted in Zara's drawing power.

My other case is the bicycle industry of contemporary Taiwan. After the Second World War, the government prohibited imports of finished bicycles and only important components of bicycles could enter the Taiwanese market. This protectionist policy fostered the emergence of the "big four" bicycle manufacturers in the 1950s: namely Ta-Tung, Taiwan Bicycle, Taiwan Mechanical, and Wu-Shuen. These manufacturers combined imported parts and other locally produced parts with their own brands. As manufacturing prospered, more and more factories other than the "big four" produced their own bicycle parts, and bicycle repair services would purchase these parts and sell in-store. They were the earliest *shanzhai* version of bicycles. Because of the popularity of these "no logo" bicycles, the "big four" fell out of business. These *shanzhai* bicycles then cooperated with many Western brand names (another OEM model) and were sold to Western countries in the 1970s. The inconsistent quality control of bicycles made these products controversial overseas and the Taiwanese manufacturers were accused of "dumping" low quality products on other countries. The Taiwanese government intervened and established quality control system in the bicycle manufacturing and improved the quality of these OEM factories. In 1985, Schwinn, the number one bicycle company in the U.S., set up its manufacturing line in Shenzhen and the Taiwanese bicycle OEM companies lost Schwinn's orders to the Chinese competitors. Therefore, the Taiwanese bicycle OEM companies made an important decision: to build its own brand name. Against such backdrop, the brands of Giant and Merida were invented and became household brand names for bicycles. They went so successful that even Schwinn went bankrupt in 1993.

Textbook economics suggest that developing countries should invest in research and innovation in key industries in order to enhance their competitive advantages. In reality, China's small-enterprise innovation in fast-fashion caters to a growing niche market among low-income classes. A few *shanzhai* enterprises, such as Tianyu Co. Ltd., have already formalized themselves after accumulating capital, knowledge and market shares. I argue that *shanzhai* should be understood in the context of Wikinomics, or global sharing and collaboration. Don Tapscott (Tapscott and Williams 2006) coined this term in his book of the same title. Wikinomics is based on four ideas: openness, peering, sharing, and acting globally. The recent popularity of mass collaboration in business can be seen as an extension of the trend in outsourcing, or externalizing formerly internal business functions to other business entities. *Shanzhai* manufacturers are sophisticated entrepreneurs who have succeeded by taking advantage of high-tech know-how, evading intellectual property rights enforcement, and democratizing technology. *Shanzhai* industries developed as the skills of Chinese system designers developed and as state-enterprises failed to institutionalize product research and development. In the absence of institutional channels, grassroots entrepreneurs created their own opportunities in product innovation and marketing. Whether these industries become regulated and institutionalized remains to be seen. What is clear is that they have changed the dynamics of China's phenomenal economic growth.

Class Exercise

1. In 2010, British Telecom (BT) issued a lawsuit against MediaTek because a subsidiary of MediaTek infringed a patent of BT in the United States. In the end, MediaTek and BT signed a reconciliation contract. If you were the role of the attorney representing BT, what strategies and compensation would you request from MediaTek? Why?

3

THE MARKET OF COUNTERFEIT GOODS

"To be counterfeited is a symptom of success, certainly. If we weren't copied and counterfeited it would mean that the Prada and Miu Miu labels weren't desirable," explains Patrizio Bertelli, the CEO of luxury brand name Prada during a media interview. The founder of Coco Chanel concurs: "Being copied is the ransom of success." Retail consultants Radha Chadha and Paul Husband have written a book (2007) for business professionals that highlights the role of fake goods in helping to spread the luxury brand cult in Asia. Though the manufacture, distribution, and retailing of counterfeit goods are illegal, it is not dysfunctional in the sense that these goods create an aura of authenticity and desirability for brand name items. This fact is not lost on the creators of brand name luxury items.

Luxury item "knockoffs" compete with brand name luxury goods. But they also buttress the market for luxury goods. To begin, counterfeit goods increase consumers' awareness about brand name goods in countries like China. By creating their own brands, counterfeiters also inject creativity, innovation, and competition into the luxury goods industry. As Shanghai furniture designer Zhengguang Ho explains, China's copy culture is like its one-child policy—a source of social disruption and an engine of economic growth. In the 30 years that have followed China's economic liberalization, Chinese consumers have cultivated a taste for luxury goods through their consumption of counterfeit products.

I mentioned in Chapter 1 that counterfeiting has long existed in human history. Nowhere is this rich history more evident than in the fashion and luxury goods industry. Throughout the 20th century, copying and counterfeiting have been constant themes in the fashion history of the West. Former American First Lady Jacqueline Kennedy was known to have satisfied her French fashion fixation by ordering from Chez Ninon, an American company that copied Paris couture. Her carefully cultivated First Lady charm hinged on her buying only from American designers and on her fashionable thriftiness for the time. This history of fashion and spendthrifts continues today in American culture. The fictional Carrie in *Sex and the City* shops for knockoffs in Los Angeles, while the popular fashion magazine *Marie Claire* features a section called "Steal" style, in which it offers tips on where to buy knockoffs of brand name items. The history of fashion is, indeed, a two-fold tale of innovation and imitation. But what do luxury goods knockoffs mean in China, where economic liberalization, central planning, and postmodern consumption collide? In the following sections, I explore what fashion has meant historically in the West and what it means to an emerging consumer culture in contemporary China.

The Rise of Brand Names

The use of clothing as a symbol of social class in Western society, and human society in general, has a long history (see Sennett 1992). Clothing often determined whom a person could approach and how they should do it. Inevitably elite fashions were copied by the masses, an imitation that further solidified the association between elite and taste, wealth and culture, status and innovation. In 17th-century Shanghai, as Jack Goody (2006) points out, fashion was one way for the rich to distinguish themselves from lower classes until the lower classes began to mimic their clothing styles.

In the West, the luxury goods industry has crafted an "aura of good taste" through advertising and marketing. It has also nurtured a feeling of intimacy between consumers and brands that serves to increase the value of luxury brand name products. The social dimension of consuming luxury brand name products is illustrated visually with showy brand name logos, which become symbols that mark one's economic and social status. In the East, luxury goods carry both social status and the message that one "belongs" to a modern, global society. In describing contemporary Asia, Chadha and Husband (2007: i) note the "secretaries toting their Burberry bags, junior executives sporting Rolex watches, and university students in Ferragamo shoes." The brand name mania in Asia, or "luxeplosion," gives new meaning to the phrase "you are what you wear" in that the brand names carry meaning about social status.

Given the growing popularity of luxury fashion in Asia, Asian markets are seen as "gold mines" for fashion companies. Luxury jewelry company Bulgari Spa, for example, saw its sales grow 19 percent in Asia outside Japan in the last quarter of 2009, a year marking a major global recession. In Japan, 40 percent of people own at least one Louis Vuitton product. Indeed, Japan accounts for 40 percent of the sales of luxury goods, compared to America's 17 percent and Europe's 16 percent. Hong Kong boasts more Gucci and Hermes stores than New York or Paris, and China and has become one of, if not the biggest, luxury product markets in the world. In total, Asian consumers account for as much as half of the $80 billion global luxury accessories industry. In China, the meaning of fashion has been influenced by the country's unique political economic history. Political leaders took fashion as an important part of the political "revolution" process. Despite Western fashion's association with Western imperialism, Chinese leaders and citizens embraced Western fashion.[1] Overseas students played a key role in this respect; they brought back Western ideas and fashions from their studying abroad experiences and influenced Chinese society in all things ideological and commercial. In the 1920s, under the leadership of United States educated Dr. Sun Yat-Sen, the Nationalist government instituted Western-style clothes as uniforms for the purpose of *shijieda-tung* (realizing peace of the world) (Bian 2007).[2] In 1925, Dr. Sun Yat-Sen turned to communism and mandated government officials wear a Chinese tunic suit, which had four patch pockets in the front.[3] This Chinese tunic quickly became China's most popular outfit of that era and was symbolically associated with the revolution. Later it was adopted by Mao Zedong and was known as the "Mao's suit." For women, the traditional *cheongsam,* a Chinese-style one-piece dress, became popular among female students in Western academies in Shanghai after 1925. The *cheongsam* remained in vogue in urban China until the early 1960s. In the United States, it was known as "Madam Chiang Kai-Shek's dress."

The People's Republic of China, which emerged after the 1949 Communist Party victory over the Chinese Nationalists, was greatly influenced by Soviet-style communism. Consequently, workers' clothing and Russian, Lenin-style suits dominated Chinese fashion until 1966.[4] When the Chinese Cultural Revolution broke out in 1966, a time that was supposed to revitalize people's commitment to the principles of the Communist Party, cosmetics, rings, bracelets, earrings, and necklaces were labeled "feudalistic" and confiscated. The Chinese Revolutionary Army uniform became the model for the period, and the Red Guard, masses mobilized by Mao Zedong consisting largely of students and other youths dressed in green military uniforms, became an icon for this period. After the Cultural Revolution (1966–1977), the green military uniform—"national defense green—continued to dominate. Even young women preferred to wear military uniforms rather than feminine clothes.

In 1979, the Chinese government's policy of rejecting a Western-style market economy began to change, along with Chinese people's lifestyles and perceptions of Western capitalism. Western fashions came to be embraced by young villagers who came of age in the 1990s, when the state worked hand-in-hand with global capitalism to promote consumerism as the new cultural ideology. The change in people's clothing embodied the increasing investment in consumerism and individualism. Jeans are an iconic example. China's youth began wearing jeans in the 1980s, and the simple Levi Strauss jeans remain popular even today. But the Chinese thirst for fashion extends far beyond jeans.

Despite the shrinking luxury goods markets globally (down 35 percent in 2008), the Chinese market for luxury goods maintains a 22 percent growth rate.

Versace hosted its first Chinese fashion show in 2008. And in January of 2009, China became the second largest consumer of luxury goods, second only to the United States. One Beijing resident, Yen, explained to me: "In China, the luxury goods create an aura for people who use them. During the economic downturn they are even more essential to cover the fact of the loss in investment." Jewelry has replaced real estate as an investment. Because of the growing investment in luxury goods in China, the Chinese government has taxed luxury goods since 2006. Cosmetics are taxed at a rate of 50 percent, golf clubs at 30 percent, watches at 30 percent, and white wine at 20 percent.

Celebration of Life Events

We know that China is fast becoming a market for luxury goods. We know that these goods carry social significance. But what exactly are the meanings that Chinese citizens attach to these goods? To investigate, I conducted focus groups and interviews with consumers in Taiwan and China. I found that luxury goods play an important role in marking major life events and coming of age moments. A blend of Chinese and Japanese traditions makes the coming of age particu-larly celebratory in contemporary Taiwan. According to a 2007 survey con-ducted by a Taiwanese fashion magazine, *Brand Magazine*, 50 percent of female readers aged 20 to 35 were gifted brand name bags when they turned 20.[5]

Chiachia Liu, a 27-year-old, confirmed the practice of giving luxury bags as coming of age gifts: "My first brand name bag was my 21st birthday gift. Of course I was happy when I received it, and many mothers of my classmates give brand name bags to their daughters as gifts, too. I don't wear it every day because it looks too mature on me, and it is too much of a show-off to bring it to school. It does not go together with my 'cute-style' clothes either." Zhiwen Huang, who grew up in Kaohsiung, the second largest city in Taiwan, was also given brand name bags as gifts. Zhiwen owns a couple of Gucci bags, gifts from her mother-in-law who runs real estate development companies. Bileen Chou, a general chief gynecologist, asked me to go shopping with her to find a pair of brand name shoes to match her wedding gown. She explained: "There are more women in this specialty [gynecology] and we spend more time discussing fash-ion." Shrugging her shoulders, she continued: "It is peer pressure."

In Taiwan, women aged 25 to 35 spend an average of NTD 20,000 to 30,000 shopping for brand name commodities every year. Before going shopping, girls do their research by reading magazines and exchanging information on the Internet. Some consumers even see brand names as "investment targets," simu-lating stocks or mutual funds that can be sold on the market at a higher price, resulting in burgeoning second-hand markets for brand name goods.

Of course, brand name hand bags and other luxury goods do more than mark major life events and investment targets. They help define elite culture and demarcate social status. On April 26, 2006, the world's largest Louis Vuitton party was held in the Chiang Kai-Shek Memorial Hall in Taipei. Said to be an ambitious attempt by Louis Vuitton in expanding its business in East Asia, Louis Vuitton purposely organized the event by social status. Guests were categorized into three groups designated to enter the venue at 9 pm, 10 pm, and 11 pm respectively. At the designated time, most guests took golf carts from the main gate of Chiang Kai-Shek Hall to their seats. Only the most famous celebrity guests were invited to enter the "VIP Boxes." The celebrities then carried their collection of brand name accessories for photographers to take glamorous shots to be reported in the newspapers the next day. In the months that followed, fashion critics commented that the party was key to Louis Vuitton's successful brand marketing. The price of a bag, US$1,000–1,500, was acclaimed by local media as "reasonably priced given their links to history and cultural meanings."

The Production of Fake Luxury Goods

The rising popularity of all things brand named has created a vast counterfeit market for brand name fashion in China. This market is organized regionally, with different provinces specializing in the manufacture of different counterfeit goods.

In Guangdong Province, clothes and middle to low-end watches are the "specialty." Adjacent Guangxi Province is also a production base for a small number of watches. Zhejiang and Jiangsu Provinces specialize in the manufacturing of counterfeit brand name bags, high-end brand name clothes and copies of cell phones. As mentioned above, these regional specialties result from different concentrations of industries in different provinces. Guangdong and Guangxi provinces have attracted low-end technology industries, whereas Jiangsu and Zhejiang Provinces are the bases for many factories producing highend electronics, textiles and garments. Putian of Fujian Province is the fake sneakers central (Schmidle 2010). In general, areas where legitimate manufacturing is concentrated are home to counterfeit factories. Depending on the specialty, the supply chain for the production of counterfeit goods can reach a national scale. In the case of counterfeit bags, clothes, watches and fake liquor, anonymity in the supply chain is strictly maintained as a way to avoid policing.

In 2009, the consumption of luxury goods grew 12 percent in China, to some $12 billion.

Because of the recent economic crisis, some producers of world-famous brand names filed for bankruptcy, including Christian Lacroix (France), Escada (Germany), and Yohji Yamamoto (Japan). Globally in 2009, the total sales of luxury brands were down 8 percent, prompting the French government to set up a "fashion bank" to support the fashion industry.

Table 3.1 **2009 Top 10 Luxury Brands**

Ranking	Brand Name	Product	Brand Value (Unit: $ billions)
1	Louis Vuitton	Purse	19.3
2	Hermes	Purse	7.48
3	Gucci	Clothes and Purses	7.46
4	Chanel	Purses	6.62
5	Rolex	Watch	5.52
6	Hennessy	Liquor	5.38
7	Cartier	Jewelry	5.19
8	Moet & Chandon	Champaign	4.84
9	Fendi	Purse	3.47
10	Prada	Clothes and Purses	2.69

Source: Forbes

But Chinese tourists in Paris were still buying so many brand name handbags that stores had to limit purchases to one bag per person. On the other hand, people from different social classes consume counterfeit products as affordable alternatives.

On January 6, 2005, someone reported to the investigative police task force on economic crime that two male suspects sold fake brandy of brand names Hennessey, Chivas, and Remy Martin at a 40 to 70 percent mark down in night-clubs and bars across the northern Chinese city of Tianjin. After a month of investigation, the task force arrested the two suspects and confiscated 4,800 bottles of fake imported liquor. The alcohol turned out to be imported from Zhongshan City in Guangdong Province, and the investigation was turned over to the Zhongshan police force.

After three months of investigation, the location and identity of the fake liquor manufacturer was finally revealed. Suspects included Sochiang Lai and seven other temporary migrant workers from the countryside of Guangdong. Lai's apartment was used as a "factory" as well as storage space for the fake brandy. The fake bottles featured laser-burned lot numbers and specialized anti-counterfeit labels, which are used on authentic imported products. Each bottle was sold at RMB 45 and earned a profit of RMB 5. Lai claimed that he purchased materials, including bottles, tags, alcohol, and packing materials from different sources and assembled the produce in his apartment. He used a soft pipe to fill the bottles and attached bottle caps manually with a cap sealer. The fake price tags came from Xantou, a city in eastern Guangdong. The alcohol was imported from Tianjin City. Bottles came from a recycler of wine bottles for clubs and bars. Lai's relatives taught him to use a pre-paid cell phone to get in touch with the suppliers of materials.

In the case of high-end fake watch production, a counterfeiter purchases real Rolex watches of lower price models, disassembles them and attaches fake diamonds to sell as an upgraded version of an authentic Rolex watch. The leftover genuine Rolex watchcase is then used to house a fake Rolex watch. Manufacturers and distributors of counterfeit watches in China classify the goods into one of four categories. A B-level product is the most common and is visibly distinguishable from genuine goods. An A-level product is not easily distinguishable from genuine goods, but the interior material and accessories are of poor quality, with easily broken clasps or easily torn interior fibers. An AA-level product is like an A-level product, but of better quality. Finally, a Super A-level product is an exact, detailed copy of the genuine item.

What are the differences between brand name goods and fake ones in terms of production? I interviewed the staff of Coach, Gucci, Chanel, Louis Vuitton, Fendi, and Prada, the most commonly counterfeited brand names, to find out. The Coach staff told me that there is no difference between high-quality imitations and the real ones. The staff of Louis Vuitton, Prada, and Chanel refused to comment. The staff of Fendi explained that there are differences in stitching, hardware, and leather accents. A real Fendi bag, for example, should have no loose or missing stitches. The color of the thread should match the main color of the bag and the stitches should be evenly spaced. If the handbag is leather, the logo should be engraved, not just printed on the leather. As well, designers almost always use leather accents, not plastic. As for Gucci, the staff

Figure 3.1 **In Yiwu's Market ("Georgi Amoni" store).**

explained that the font curves of a real Gucci bag should be exactly the same as the picture on Gucci's official website, with no grammatical or spelling errors. If the "G" looks more like an "E," it is a fake. The E-like logo is the most common way to counterfeit a Gucci. There are also differences in dust covers, color, and stitching between the authentic and the counterfeit.

Many manufacturers, including Fendi, Dior, Gucci, Kate Spade and Coach, use authenticity cards to mark an authentic product. An authenticity card usually has the manufacturer's logo embossed on the front and has information about the product. Sometimes these cards will have a magnetic strip or bar code. Some counterfeiters, however, also attach fake authenticity cards to their bags. Obvious mistakes in spelling and grammar are used to avoid flagrant intellectual property rights violations. For instance, ELLE might be spelled EFFE.

Large profits in the counterfeit business provide an incentive to invest in counterfeiting, especially since the penalties pale in comparison to the profits. In addition, the separate jurisdictions and laws between Mainland China and Hong Kong and Taiwan have made it easy for counterfeiters to operate from a distance. One counterfeiter kept a residence in Hong Kong near the Chinese border and would simply drive across the border each morning to his illegal factory in Shenzhen. In the evening, he would return to the protective sanctuary of Hong Kong. His factory is staffed by local Chinese, who are all "too eager to work in a lucrative trade at a time when unemployment and layoffs are common among China's legitimate enterprises" (Chow 2003: 474–475). In the next chapter, I will discuss the intricate networks that support the distribution of counterfeit goods.

Class Exercise

1. "You are what you wear": Choices of clothes, accessories or even cell phones also have social meanings. Discuss with two or three other classmates the "price" you are willing to pay for consuming counterfeit products of brand names. What are the meanings of your wearing "counterfeit accessories?"

4

CONSUMING COUNTERFEIT GOODS

This chapter aims to delineate the supply chain and markets for counterfeit goods. As I will show, this is a global market that is at once quite visible and "under the table." Distributors and retailers go to great lengths to market and transport counterfeit items under the radar and to avoid detection by the authorities. In turn, the regulatory sectors of China and Taiwan have innovated new ways of pursuing counterfeiters, or at least creating the illusion that they are pursuing intellectual property right violations for trademark holders. In addition to describing the very vibrant markets for counterfeit goods, I examine the consumption of fake goods and their meaning to consumers around the world.

The Supply and Distribution of Counterfeits

Having delineated how counterfeit goods are made, I now turn my attention to how fake products are supplied to retailers and consumers. Counterfeit goods find their way out of China and into foreign cities via cargo ships, air, and, increasingly, through the internet. According to an anonymous officer who works for the Chinese Directorate General of Customs, Taiwan used to be—but is no longer—a transferring port for counterfeit goods exported from China. Once centered in Taiwan, the ports have since moved to Southeast Asia and Hong Kong. To avoid detection, the goods are shipped through these ports to a third country, such as Italy, where they acquire formal documents and invoices. Thus, in customs, there have been cases of counterfeit goods that are "Made in Italy," or "Made in Japan."[1]

Fishing boats and cargo ships carrying counterfeit goods from North Korea, China, Vietnam, and the Philippines also circle around the seas of East and Southeast Asia looking for chances to sell their stock. Often, Taiwanese merchants will receive orders in Taiwan but manufacture the products in China, which they then sell overseas. When counterfeit goods are found in cargo that is making a transferring stop in Taiwan, customs have no right to confiscate the material, but they still notify the trademark owner. Even so, it is impossible for customs to search through all incoming and outgoing cargos.

Typically, counterfeit goods are manufactured in China, exported to Taiwanese wholesalers, and sold through anonymous websites, boutique shops, second hand shops, and television shopping channels. The ET Mall television channel pre-ordered 200 brand name bags from a merchant who ran a boutique shop in Shindien, Taipei. Each bag costs NTD 7,000, about 20–30 percent lower than the same items sold in the store. The ET Mall found the goods suspicious and asked the authorities to check them out. It turned out that the bags were fake copies. The merchant knew the supplier from Singapore, but, when the counterfeiting was discovered, could not reach him. The authorities could do little to help the merchant because the trade in counterfeiting is not considered an international crime.

Counterfeit goods are also transported by air. At the airport, customs officers try to distinguish between counterfeit importers and ordinary travelers, as well as between real and counterfeit goods. Some corporations even have special training sessions for customs officials to teach them how to distinguish real from fake stuff. Cizhi Chen, a counterfeit vendor in Taichung, had just turned 19 and got into the business part time when I interviewed him in 2007. During his summer vacation, Cizhi had worked in a relative's glass-making factory to earn pocket money and save for school tuition. But he discovered that selling counterfeit goods earned better income than a factory job. His friend, A-ho Tsai, ordered goods in Shenzhen or Korea once or twice a month, which are shipped to Taiwan by airmail. A-ho rented studios near Feng-Chia Market to store the goods. Whenever Cizhi received an order from his friends, he would call A-ho, pick up the goods from the storage studio, and deliver the goods to the buyer by motorcycle. All communications are made by cell phone to avoid police.

The scale of the customs operation is impressive. In 2009 alone, Hong Kong airport authority confiscated 510,000 counterfeit items. Sixty percent of them were fake cell phones, accessories, electronic products and personal computers outbound to Middle East, South Asia, and South America and 56,000 pieces of fake brand clothes were confiscated.

As far as Cizhi knows, there is no factory in Taiwan that manufactures counterfeit bags. About 80 percent of the bags come from Mainland China; the remaining 20 percent come from Korea. Each bag costs NTD 200–300 and is sold at NTD 1,000 or more, making his monthly income between US$10 and $300.

The fake producers use two types of marketing strategies. The first type is direct mail. Direct mail is the delivery of advertising materials to recipients of postal mails. Counterfeiters avoid police investigations by delivering product catalogues to mailboxes, flyers attached to newspaper deliveries, or randomly giving out catalogues on busy streets to potential customers. To avoid police investigations, counterfeiters usually pay people, who are unaware of the illegal nature of the business, to apply for the cell phone numbers listed in the catalogues.

Many counterfeiting operations are conducted over the internet, which complicates the detection of trademark violations and the enforcement of intellectual property rights since it requires international police cooperation. Before China's Xiangyang Market closed in 2006, an online version of the market had its grand opening. The website offers a navigating map of the real Xiangyang Market with icons for each shop in English, Japanese, and Chinese. Clicking on the icons results in a pop-up window with the shop's name and a variety of counterfeit goods on display.

In addition to the online Xiangyang Market, counterfeit goods are sold over the internet through online auction sites or spam mails. Anonymous sellers, for example, will often use legal auction sites like Taobao, an online auction site similar to eBay.[2] One informant sold ten items in the first month, but ten items a day in the second month. "Chinese people now shop online," she explained. Authorized payments and receipts are ensured by a Chinese e-commerce business similar to PayPal, a payment intermediary service that facilitates e-commerce. The recipient of a PayPal transfer can request a check from PayPal, establish their own PayPal deposit account or request a transfer to their bank account.

In 2007, The Louis Vuitton Group (LVMH) sued eBay for 37 million Euros for allowing the sale of counterfeit goods. The suit estimated that 90 percent of the sales of Louis Vuitton on eBay involve counterfeits. eBay, however, has no policy to remove sales unless it is proven that they involve counterfeits, and long legal processes are necessary to make such an appraisal.

The Marketing and Retail of Counterfeit Goods

Each counterfeit market is deeply embedded in local networks and cultures. In this section, I explore counterfeit markets in five major places: Shenzhen, Shanghai, Yiwu, Taiwan, and New York.

Shenzhen

At 355.8 meters in height with 75 floors, Seg was once the tallest steel-reinforced concrete building and the first skyscraper in Shenzhen. The first nine floors featured retail and wholesale markets for electronics; the remaining floors contained office space, a hotel, an observatory, and maintenance and helicopter taxi areas. Meijuan Guo sold brand name cell phones at the Seg Market. The shop next to hers sold fake Apple iPods, with the Apple icon reversed and "MP4" inscribed on the back instead of "I-P-O-D." Next to the fake Apple shop was a fake watch shop, with imitation brand name watches featuring similar but different names, such as "Eagle" for "Omega." In the back of the mall, Wü—an imitation of the Nintendo Wii game system—accessories are sold at shops near the narrow escalators. Each shop has two to three clerks attending customers in a space of less than one square meter. One counterfeit shopkeeper estimated that the majority of her customers were from the United States.

Meijuan took me to Luohu Commercial City and East Gate Mall to see other counterfeit vendors. Luohu Commercial City at Luohu train station is a six-story mall with many small shops. Each floor had approximately 80 to 100 shops selling bags, shoes, textiles, video games and accessories, snacks, tea, and medicine alongside foot massage salons and nail salons. East Gate Mall, an area near Laojie subway station, supplies counterfeit luxury goods at a much higher price. In all the markets, the counterfeit goods were often hidden. Customers would browse through catalogues, go to a storage place with the shop owners, and then return to the shops to arrange for payments over the table.

Renting a space at Luohu Mall is no small cost. To avert rent costs, many counterfeit retailers had devised a new sales system. A telephone number would be given to potential customers to make an appointment to meet at the Starbucks near Luohu train station. After confirming that the customer was not an undercover police officer, the customer would be directed to locked warehouses in the train station, where counterfeit goods would be on display. This new sales pattern had the added benefit of lowering the risks of being caught by the police, though it imposed something of a safety risk for both sellers and buyers. In the trade of counterfeit goods, salespeople generally have contact with one or two suppliers. The supplier, in turn, would have contact with the manufacturer. The separation of retailer and manufacturer provided some protection to the manufacturer should the retailer be caught.

The nature of illegality has made the counterfeiting business heavily reliant on personal networking. Qiuyi Wu, a businessman who has run a business in Shenzhen for 20 years, summarizes three key elements to operating a counterfeit operation in Shenzhen: (1) conduct your trade in cash; (2) maintain connections with police and officials; and (3) keep a good relationship with the Chaozhou gang, a nickname for people who were born in Chaozhou, a city located in Northeast Guangdong Province. For instance, a friend of Qiuyi opened an outlet store for counterfeit computer products in a mall in Shenzhen several years ago. As soon as the store started to make money, the mall manager, a Chaozhou native, raised his rent. Once Qiuyi's friend left, the Chaozhou native opened a similar store at the same address. Basically, the Chaozhou native usurped Qiuyi's friend's business.

Qiuyi Wu then explained that in the underground economy, success depended on connections or unwritten, verbal contracts. However, bonds of clanships seem to prevail currently.

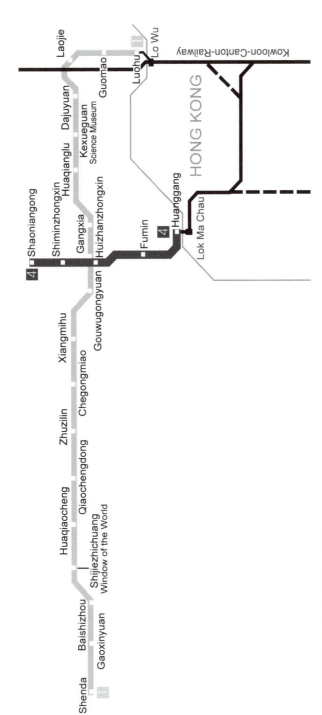

Figure 4.1 **Shenzhen's Subway Map.**

Figure 4.2 **A Glance at Tourists in the Luohu Mall.**

Shanghai

In Shanghai, China's largest city, markets, international business and tourism intersect to create a fast-paced urban landscape. Once a fishing town, Shanghai was opened as a port city in the 19th century, after which it flourished as a hub of commerce and finance between East and West. In 2005, Shanghai became the world's busiest cargo port.

One local estimated that the first open air counterfeit market, Huating Road Market, opened around 1993. Vendors set up stands on both sides of the Huating Road and hailed customers on the street. In 2000, another counterfeit market—Xiangyang Market—was opened. In the beginning, few customers patronized the market. The municipal government of Shanghai then forced vendors to move their stalls from Huating Street Market to Xiangyang Market, making it more popular among Shanghai citizens. During weekdays, some 15,000 visitors made their way to the market on any given day. But during national holidays, as many as 20,000 to 30,000 visitors crowded around the vendors. In 2002, the rent for one vendor unit surged from RMB 3,000 to RMB 18,000 per month. Xiangyang Market specialized in two types of goods: counterfeit goods and ethnic goods.

Xiangyang Market was permanently closed in 2006. Locals spread the rumor that it was closed due to the pressure from the U.S. government because of intellectual property rights violations. In fact, the market was relocated in order to construct high-rise buildings for sale.

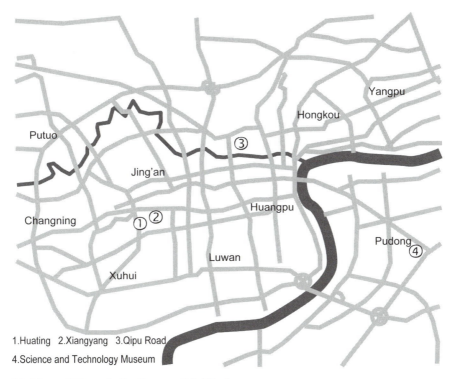

1.Huating   2.Xiangyang   3.Qipu Road
4.Science and Technology Museum

Figure 4.3 **Map of Shanghai's Counterfeit Markets.**

Figure 4.4 **The Underground Mall at Shanghai's Science and Technology Museum.**

Figure 4.5 **Posters of Regulations of Marketplaces and Brand Name's Authenticity Checklist at Shanghai.**

Today, the sale of counterfeit goods is concentrated in three places: Yatai Shenghui Mall, Qipu Road, and Email Fashion Department Store. A few counterfeiters also hire people to hang around the old Xiangyang Market site to solicit business. Interested customers are then taken to nearby apartments where counterfeit goods are sold. Operated by the Shanghai Municipal Government, Yatai Shenghui is an underground mall with a capacity for more than 100 shops. It is located at the exit of the Science and Technology Museum Metro station. In some of the shops, storage is hidden above the ceiling for stocking goods, including counterfeit bags. Most foreign shoppers favor this mall because it supplies catalogues of brand name goods and their unauthorized copies.

Qipu Road is a shopping zone located in Hongkuo District near an area that was once a Jewish refugee settlement during the Second World War. Today, the area is dominated by mainly Chinese shoppers who visit the shopping malls on Qipu Road. Counterfeit goods here are considered of lesser quality than those in the Yatai Shenghui Mall. Finally, Email Fashion Department Store is located at Jinganshi Metro station, only a few blocks away from a new Japanese department store and the high-end shopping area of Nanjing West Road. Email Fashion Department Store only carries goods for women.

Many vendors in Shanghai boasted that their goods represented overstock of real brand name factories or were manufactured in Korea, known as producing better quality products than China. In fact, most of the goods are counterfeits and are manufactured in China. Some of these goods are of higher quality than others, with a range of prices reflecting the range in quality. Prices were also determined by the perceived wealth of the customer. One shop owner in Yatai Shenghui admitted that she would sell a pair of fake boots to a Shanghainese for RMB 300–600, but would immediately raise the price to RMB 1,000 if the customer were "a blonde."

Yiwu

Located on the Eastern end of Jin-Qu Basin in Zhejian Province, Yiwu has under its jurisdiction 15 towns and eight villages. In 2007, Yiwu had a population of 650,000. As an inland city, Yiwu is connected to the Shanghai Economic Zone to the North by a bullet train that takes two hours. The train station was always packed with migrant workers and business people who had just arrived or were leaving for a home visit. In 1995, Yiwu ranked 47th among China's 100 most powerful cities regarding comprehensive economic strength. And, since 2001, Yiwu's small commodity market model has topped China's 100 top open markets.[3] There are 12 small commodity markets in Yiwu, each selling one particular type of commodity. They include such markets as the central Zhejiang wood market and the central Zhejiang manufacturing material market. These markets are located in modernist-style concrete buildings. With two exceptions, the markets are two to three storeys in height. The first floor is typically the shop floor, and the second floor is usually used for storage of raw materials. Once an order is placed, the vendor will run to the storage area to acquire the raw material, returning to what is typically a family run workshop where they will start work immediately. For knitting, which requires more intensive labor, the shop owners will typically outsource to workers in Dongyang City, which is about 15 minutes away.

In addition to retail markets, Yiwu features wholesale markets, which are established and operated by the local government out of the Administration of Industry and Commerce (AIC). AICs are charged with policing counterfeit operations, as well as with collecting fees from individual wholesalers, which can easily exceed $100,000 per year (Chow 2003). In Yiwu, wholesale prices for small goods are particularly cheap because the suppliers come from family workshops that compete fiercely with one another. With its inexpensive goods, Yiwu has become the shopping haven for tourists and global merchants. The languages spoken in the city include Korean, Arabic, Mandarin, Zhejiang dialect, English, Hindu, Spanish, and a few others I could not identify. "The Korean merchants are the most difficult to deal with," claimed Jingqi Zhang, a native of Yiwu, who was my local guide. Jingqi was the owner of a small workshop that manufactures belts for export. Here, in Yiwu, most of the counterfeit goods are bound for export. "Local people are not interested in brand names," Jingqi explained. Yiwu also supplies good for Japanese "100 yen stores" (comparable to the U.S. dollar store) and the American seasonal gift market. The number of 100 yen stores in Japan has reached 150,000 in recent years, creating increased demand for cheap goods imported from Yiwu (Sakamoto 2008). In addition, business with the Middle East is tremendous. Some 90 percent of Yiwu exports go to the Middle East (Li and Zhang 2002). Jingqi knew of one Middle East merchant who would order goods at a rate of seven cargo containers per day.

Yiwu got its nickname as the "Counterfeit Capital" from U.S. television company CBS. Counterfeit goods are scattered in shops at the International Trade Mart malls and in other retail shops on the streets of Yiwu. Although Jinqi does not make copies of brand name items, he knows people who do and who export to Central and South America. He emphasized that the mostly foreign exporters earn more than the locals because they are experienced traders who have extensive international networks.

At the age of 70, Cunzhi Chiang, from Taiwan, has run multiple businesses in Yiwu for ten years. She worked in Japan in her 20s and 30s, and later she immigrated to Brazil. Her three sons now run a major supermarket chain in Brazil that has expanded to a few other countries in South America. Cunzhi and her husband relocated to China in 1998 as representatives of the procurement

Figure 4.6 **A "*Shanzhai*" Sneaker Store at Yiwu.**

department for their sons. She spends about 200 days a year working in Yiwu to supply toys and other small commodities to the South American market. During the rest of the year, she reunites with her husband who is based in Guangdong and in charge of the procurement of bags, accessories and other goods. She ships 20 cargo containers to Brazil every month. Cunzhi uses the living room of her apartment as office space, and I caught a glimpse of her Spartan bedroom when we spoke. Cunzhi said that she did not deal in the counterfeiting trade and always made sure that trademarked goods were authorized. "However, not every exporter reveals the origin of their goods," she explained. She pointed to the boxes of goods stacked ready to be shipped to South America, which blocked the entrance to her fellow trader's apartment next door.

Taiwan

Taiwan, an island off the Southeast coast of mainland China and also known as the Republic of China as distinct from the People's Republic of China, emerged after the civil war in which the forces of Mao Zedong defeated Chiang Kai-shek in 1949. In the 1980s, Taiwan became the base of counterfeit production due to its cheaper labor and geographical proximity to Japan, which is a source of much of the demand for counterfeit merchandise. According to Chang (2004), counterfeits were made in Taiwan until the real brand name companies started to expand their businesses to Taiwan. In the 1990s, counterfeiters made China their new production base, and today more than 90 percent of the counterfeit goods confiscated in Taiwan are made in China or Korea. Taichung and Taipei cities were the two places I studied counterfeit activities in Taiwan. In 2009, Taipei City had a population of 2,607,428. It features two major counterfeit markets: the Dinghao market zone, located near a major department store in downtown; and Wufenpu market, which has no high-end department stores nearby. In Dinghao market zone, counterfeit bags are sold at "second-hand" boutique shops. Other counterfeiters make catalogues and avoid police by delivering packages to regular customers.

Taichung is the third-largest city in Taiwan with the highest income per capita. Taichung's population is now just over one million and includes workers who come from neighboring counties to work in Taichung's manufacturing and high-tech industries. One of Taichung's major counterfeit markets is the Fengchia Market, which operates from 7 pm to midnight seven days a week. Night markets are hotbeds for counterfeit sales. They appeal to lower-income customers and police patrols take place less frequently. In the 1980s, the sales of illegal items in the night market were largely pirated cassettes and CDs of popular songs, as well as pirated Hollywood movies. Counterfeit clothes, bags and watches could also be found from time to time in the markets. Taichung's other counterfeit market, Jingming 1st Street, is located in a shopping area two blocks away from a Louis Vuitton flagship store and two high-end department stores. Individual street vendors in this market sell hairpins, fashion accessories, clothes, and counterfeit bags.

New York

According to the United States Customs and Border Protection, in Fiscal Year (FY) 2008, the value of goods seized for intellectual property rights (IPR) violations increased by 39 percent to US$272.7 million (up from $196.7 million in FY 2007). The number of IPR seizures increased by 9.7 percent. China was the top trading partner for IPR seizures, accounting for 81 percent of the total value in counterfeit goods seized. Footwear was the top commodity seized and accounted for 38 percent of the entire value of illegal goods seized. Counterfeit pharmaceuticals and accessories had also increased more than 100 percent in domestic value between FY 2007 and 2008.

New York State is home to 12 percent of the U.S. counterfeit goods trade, and New York City alone is home to 8 percent (Padavan 2005a).[4] There are local laws to regulate the selling of counterfeit goods on New York City streets (See Duneier 1999; Stoller 2006), but many unauthorized street vendors sell counterfeit goods near major department stores. Although the illegal vendors benefit from sales to tourists, the city's residents are deprived of sales tax revenue. In 2003, the estimated unpaid sales tax on counterfeit goods was US$380 million; the unpaid business taxes on the production and sale of counterfeit goods was US$290 million; and the unpaid personal income tax was US$360 million (Padavan 2005a). Compared to the smuggling of drugs, counterfeit goods' importation enjoyed low penalties while profits were high (Schmidle 2010).

Not far away from the Herald Square shops and Fashion Avenue, in the shadows of the famous Garment District, sits the Broadway strip, what police call "Counterfeit Alley." Counterfeiters use the old office buildings in midtown for storage and to conduct wholesale business. The counterfeiters wait at the building entrances muttering questions like "CDs? Sneakers? Chanel?" Tourists and residents sometimes call these shops the "poor man's shopping mall," where lower-income families from North Carolina or Pennsylvania can afford Christmas gifts. Between 2004 and 2006, 15 old office buildings were shut down to slow the rampant counterfeiting business. The legitimate shop owners in this area shrugged their shoulders and seemed to care less about being labeled "Counterfeit Alley." One said: "For me, they find a living, I find a living; you know what I mean? You don't know if it's real or not."

On November 12, 2007, Claire Chen, a senior news reporter, accompanied police officers from Midtown Precinct North and Allegiance Protection, a private investigation company to visit a midtown warehouse of knockoff wholesalers. They found 500,000 pieces of fake bags, watches, and shoes, amounting to hundreds of thousands of US dollars. According to the arrested 19-year-old Chinese seller, they were to be sold to the Chinese or African vendors who retail these goods at Times Square, Rockefeller Center, South Street, and other places.

In *Money Has No Smell* (2002), an ethnography of African vendors in New York City, Paul Stoller observes that the informal, relational contracts that characterize the informal economy are embedded in the city's complicated transnational networks and ethnic diversity. Stoller describes accompanying his informant, Boubē, to conduct business with his Taiwanese and Korean watch wholesalers. Because he was white, Stoller was not trusted by the Taiwanese supplier until he proved that he could speak Boubē's language:

> This fragility requires a bond of unflagging trust between economic partners, a trust that, given the conditions of informality in New York City trading, frequently transcend sociocultural and national boundaries.
> (Stoller 2002: 62)

Tourists from Canada, Europe, and even Asia also buy unauthorized counterfeits from the traders on the sidewalks of Manhattan's Canal Street, and at the cross-streets of West Lafayette Avenue and Mulberry Street. A headcount in 2007 revealed that there were eight counterfeit goods sellers on one side and five on the other along this section of Canal Street. One team of sellers showcased a one-page catalogue with photos of different bags folded into the pocket of the vendor, who whispered brand names to passersby until a customer stopped and queried. The vendors took interested customers into a storage space on a back street.

The Chinatown counterfeit business has been a constant struggle between the municipal government and traders. Several informants suggested that gang organizations based on clans backed up the counterfeit business in Chinatown. Others indicated that the high rent in this district accounted for the rise of counterfeiting. In 2008 alone, more than 100 counterfeit shops were shut down in Chinatown. Counterfeiters in New York often purchase vans as mobile retail shops. "A second-hand van is cheaper than the rent of a shop anyway," one counterfeiter explained. For instance, a landlord might charge US$50,000 for one shop space on contract, but if the shop attracted many customers, they might increase the rent the following year.

Policing Counterfeiters

The United States and brand name companies have contended that a major loophole in intellectual property rights (IPR) protection is the absence of criminal sanctions for retailers in China. In fact, there are criminal sanctions for retailers in China. In 2004, the Supreme People's Court and the Supreme People's Procuratorate of the People's Republic of China clarified these sanctions. According to the judgment, criminal prosecutions may be pursued against retailers, but only if a vendor is found to have sold or offered for sale counterfeit goods in an amount that exceeds a designated threshold (RMB 50,000 or about US$6,300). The United States sought support from the World Trade Organization (WTO) in lowering this threshold, but the WTO did not support the United States in its January 2009 meeting.

Another obstacle in regulating and containing China's counterfeit trade is what Chow (2003) calls "local protectionism." Local protectionism refers to the efforts of local governments to protect local counterfeiting operations given their importance to local economic activity. These efforts may involve the imposition of light fines and penalties, which masquerade as a form of regulation but do little to deter counterfeiting (Chow 2003: 474). By protecting illegal activity through lax policies and a lack of enforcement, local protectionism preserves the local economy and protects local interests, often at the expense of national interests. In addition, the power and resources of local governments are consolidated in this way. In China, local government authorities compete with government authorities at higher administrative levels for power and resources. They also compete with government authorities in other localities in terms of economic investment and growth.[5] In the end, the drive to protect local economic interests acts as a disincentive to police and penalize counterfeiting operations.

None of this is to say that crackdowns on counterfeiting do not occur. Brand name companies Burberry, Gucci, Chanel, Louis Vuitton and Prada sued the Beijing Silk Street Company and individual vendors at the Silk Market for trademark violations in 2005 and again in 2007. The Beijing Local Court ruled that market vendors and market managers pay RMB 100,000 (US$14,718) in penalties be paid to the trademark holders. And, as part of a court-mediated agreement, the market's managers agreed to punish offending vendors by shutting down six to eight stalls for up to a week. Finally, in an effort to show its determination to create a positive image, the Silk Street Market Company unveiled its own brand—Silkstreet—in 2008 in an attempt to replace the counterfeit materials before the opening of the Beijing Olympics. Some have suggested that Shanghai's Xiangyang Market, one of the most prominent counterfeit markets in China, was forced to shut down due to anti-counterfeiting pressure from the United States.[6]

Sometimes, it is difficult for investigators to distinguish the real and the fake. In 2008 in Hangzhou, a city famous for quality textiles in Central China, a real Louis Vuitton store was shut down by government officials due to a "tag" problem. In China, the State Administration for Industry and Commerce recommends that leather manufacturers attach a tag explaining the material used in the production of each leather product. There is no such rule, however, in France. Thus, the real made-in-France Louis Vuittion bags violated Chinese law. The 600 bags confiscated were burned by government officials.

In any case, counterfeiting merchants have gone to great lengths to circumvent these crackdowns. One licensed tour guide in Beijing named Qicun Wu contended that counterfeit sellers and tourism agencies have conspired to create a clandestine nighttime market in counterfeit goods for tourists. In this market, sellers bring goods to hotel rooms where tourists may peruse and purchase the counterfeit items. In Shenzhen, I observed that shop owners had elaborated various means to guard counterfeit shops.[7] An extra pair of hands is hired regularly to carry any evidence of counterfeiting away from the shops before the police visit. During one surprise raid by the police, I witnessed young clerks carrying away bags of catalogues of fake goods to avert police investigation. As Bob Barchiesi, the president of the International Anti-counterfeiting Coalition told a fellow at the New America Foundation, Nicolas Schmidle, factory raids conducted by Chinese authorities are "propaganda shows" (Schmidle 2010). Thus, China's local governments have an ambivalent and contradictory role in policing the counterfeit markets. They are at once regulators and protectors.

I visited the headquarters of the Intellectual Property Rights Protecting Corps of Special Police (IPRP) in China to collect information about the enforcement of intellectual property laws in 2007. A guard at the front gate directed me to the first floor of the back building to see Officer Zhiwei Chen,[8] with whom I had an appointment. Much to my surprise, there was no one in the office. I walked up to the fourth floor and finally heard some voices. Ten or more officers were busy moving hundreds of plastic bags of counterfeit clothes into a storage room. After half an hour, Zhiwei emerged with dust and sweat on his face, explaining that he and his squad had just come back from confiscating a shipment of counterfeit clothes of famous American brands.

Needless to say, violating a trademark is a violation of criminal law in the Republic of China. Intellectual property rights (IPR) regulations include a copyright act, a trademark act, and a patent act. Since 1992, district public prosecutors' offices have assigned prosecutors to specifically take charge of IPR cases. And since 1999, the Ministry of Justice has designated the Taipei, Banciao, Taichung, and Kaohsiung Prosecutors Offices to set up IPR ad hoc sections aimed at increasing the prosecutors' skills and capabilities to deal with such cases. In 2000, Intellectual Property Rights Protecting Corps of Special Police (IPRP) was first staffed with 100 police officers to combat computer software piracy as a special task force. One year later, the IPRP started regular crackdowns of intellectual property violations in the night markets. In 2003, the IPRP staff increased to 220 officers to handle patent infringement cases. The IPRP is evaluated for promotion and bonus rewards according to the numbers of cases discovered, which serves to motivate the prosecution of the counterfeit goods dealer.

Pressure from the United States remains another strong motivation for the intellectual property police to improve their performance. Until 2003, Taiwan was on the priority list of the Special 301 Watch List of the United States.[9] Every year, the Intellectual Property Office of the Ministry of Economic Affairs (MOEA) in Taiwan sets up explicit goals and deadlines for actions to enforce intellectual property laws. Every three months, intellectual property officers gather at a meeting to evaluate their progress. Public procurators also meet every three months in the Higher Court and hold a meeting with Intellectual Property Police and the Executive Yuan. Presently, the Intellectual Property office focuses on the violation of copyright and trademark acts. Certain consulting companies also collect information about counterfeiters and report to the district attorneys for formal prosecution.[10]

Foreign name brands are not the only victims of trademark violation crimes. For domestic trademark violation, the problem is partly due to the structure of the Chinese language: different characters may have the same phonetic sounds, and vice versa. Counterfeiters take advantage of the language by using characters similar to those of brand names, such as Dinqinfeng for Dintaifeng. (The latter is a famous restaurant.) This has made it difficult to prosecute trademark violations in some cases. A rice ball maker was sued because its trademark, "The Third Great Uncle," a common kinship appellation, was already registered.

Timing in trademark registration is important. One local company, Jump, managed to win its trademark violation case against international shoemaker Adidas because Adidas was late in registering its trademark in Taiwan.

Daniel Chow contends that the different juridical systems in place in China, Taiwan and Hong Kong account for some of the lawlessness surrounding counterfeiting. In Taiwan, there has been much improvement in the enforcement of and the number of IPR violation cases. The success of Taiwanese police in eradicating different forms of IPR violations suggests that counterfeiting is not inherent in Chinese culture but rather a matter of education and enforcement. The IPRP indicated that the difficulty lies in a lack of coordination between countries. One major trademark holder hires ten investigation companies to assist them in enforcing intellectual property rights in China. But unless the Chinese government takes action, they cannot shut down counterfeit sales.

In her ethnographic examination of the Tibetan music industry, Morcom (2008) points out that the major problems with IPR breaches in China are corruption, lack of enforcement, and bureaucratic structure. She explains:

> [In China] the National Copyright Bureau is subordinate to the National Press and Publications Bureau (PPB), and on the provincial level, the copyright departments are contained within the PPBs. The PPB, however, is concerned mainly with censorship and has no interest in promoting the rights of authors or creating freedom in publishing so copyright retains a low priority . . . this inadequate administrative apparatus is itself a symptom of the fact that copyright and other IPR protection is not a political or national priority for China.[11]
>
> (Morton 2008: 272)

Yuying Zhou, a lawyer for an internationally renowned trademark company holds that regulating counterfeiting runs counter to our universal desire for cheap bargains. As such, she contends that, "We can never stop this kind of economic crime but we can reduce it to a smaller scale so that they do not take place right in store's fronts."

Yuying identified the counterfeiters as less educated, of a lower socioeconomic status, and coming from China's poorer regions.

In one case Yuying encountered in Taichung in 2007, the convicted counterfeiters were a struggling married couple with three young children. Customs confiscated their counterfeit goods and the Taichung Local Court sentenced the couple to 30 days in prison or a fine of NTD 30,000. With the help of volunteer legal counsel, the couple testified to their poor financial status and provided medical documentation of the husband's diagnosis of major depression. During the first trial, the judge ruled that the convicted should settle out of court with Yuying's client, but the district attorney appealed to the Higher Court. Before the second trial, the husband committed suicide. The wife, who had to attend the second trial, was sentenced to four years in prison.

Consuming Counterfeit Goods

Culture filters our perceptions of what constitutes good or responsible consumption. But as Belk, Devinney and Eckhardt (2005) discovered, affluence and past affiliation with ethical groups are better predictors of the consumer's ethical stance than culture. My interviews with consumers suggested that only a small number of consumers expressed feelings of shame for buying fake products; most of them fingered the brand names as unethical.

Arjun Appadurai has suggested that anthropologists should treat consumption as an aspect of the overall political economy of societies. For Appadurai, consumption emerges as:

> a function of a variety of social practices and classifications, rather than a mysterious emanation of human needs, a mechanical response to social manipulation or the narrowing down of a universe and voracious desire for objects to whatever happens to be available.
>
> (Appadurai 1986: 29)

From the perspective of political economy, there is certainly more at stake in buying counterfeit goods than a mere exchange of cash for goods. If the manufacturers and distributors are selective and laborious about marketing products to consumers, so are the consumers in purchasing the goods that they need and/or desire. I examine consumption from the perspective of the residents from different social backgrounds. I focus on the feelings that consumers attach to counterfeit goods and brand name products.[12]

A Quest for Otherness

This type of counterfeit consumer refers to tourists who purchase counterfeit gifts exclusively for themselves. 36-year-old Jimou Chen from California visited Yatai Shenghui in May 2008 during his visit to China. A recent immigrant to the U.S. of Taiwanese origin and a college professor, he got a local contact of a counterfeit retailer through his sister and was shown a "shoppers' heaven," to use his words. But he only bought a belt with RMB 10 with no inscribed brand name because he "could not find what he like[d]." Julie is a 32-year-old full time Taiwanese businesswoman who received a degree in Tourism. She visits Shanghai as a getaway every six months during her paid vacation days. She explained: "Shopping for counterfeit goods is always on my must-do list in Shanghai. It is a very relaxing activity."

The sense of fashion and affordability are the main reasons that young customers are drawn to counterfeit goods. In her twenties, Jingyi Li went to Shenzhen from Taiwan in 2006 to shop with her classmates as a weekend getaway vacation. Before the trip, Jingyi surfed the Internet for good places to shop for counterfeit goods. She even knew where to buy nicer and less expensive counterfeit items:

> People buy counterfeit because it's cheap and it's worth it. Geographically speaking, in Huachangbei area, which is near East Gate (all at Laojie subway station) counterfeit goods are more expensive. In Luohu area, the counterfeit goods are cheaper.

Jingyi explained to me that she attaches a different social function to each of her bags:

> My friends and I distinguish the bags' purposes according to the occasion: for some of us, brand name bags are used exclusively on a date or for work. If you go shopping during the weekend or dine near your home, you use "non-brand-name, ordinary bags."

Jingyi's classmate, Wencheng Xie, shopped for counterfeits of Japanese and European brand names because she loved both the "sense of class" and "cute culture" that those goods embody.[13] She said:

> I was not interested in buying counterfeit but I was surprised when I saw these bags. They looked just like real ones, and I thought that it is worth using them. Our friend bought toys and stuffed animals, such as Disney toys, and Japanese animation characters. I regretted that I did not buy them after seeing his purchases. I just love cute culture!

For this type of consumer, fake goods satisfy their desire for foreign brand names.

Consumption as Sociality

Another type of counterfeit consumer consists of business travelers who buy fake products as gifts for family members at home. Mr. Tanaka, a 70-year-old Japanese businessman, said that in the 1980s he regularly visited Taipei, purchased fake Rolex watches in the back streets and brought them back as souvenirs for friends in Japan. Ken, a U.S. citizen of Middle Eastern origin, mentioned that he used to shop for fake watches in batches in Korea and brought them back to the United States as gifts in the 1990s.

Yoyi Chen, the department head of a major manufacturing unit in his late 30s offered that each time before he takes a trip to Taiwan, he emails his relatives and friends with the latest catalogues supplied by counterfeit watches and bag sellers and takes orders for them. Yoyi showed off his "Rolex" watch: "This is the finest quality and I got it for only RMB 300." Likewise, a graduate student studying in the United States, Shufeng Lin, purchased fake socks, bags and watches as gifts for friends and family in Taiwan during a trip to China.

Juoqin Wang was a regular shopper at Xiaohong's fake purse shop in Shenzhen Luohu Mall. She showed off her "Hermès" purse and "Chanel" bag. A 31-year-old businesswoman with a master's degree in Business Administration from a U.S. university, she demonstrated a sophisticated understanding of counterfeit manufacturing and its relation to brand name manufacturing:

> French brands such as Hermès and Chanel are the best candidates for counterfeiting because these two brands use leather for the materials of their bags. Leather products are easier to copy as long as you have good sources for quality raw material. An AA fake producer processes leather purses according to the standard operation protocol of the brand name factory. On the other hand, copying an American brand such as Coach presents more difficulty for counterfeiters because Coach bags use more non-leather fabrics that require complicated processes of dying or stitching. The counterfeiters would not want to waste time and money in research and design in this regard. Counterfeiters would only make the ones for mass production instead of those of limited edition and handcrafted bags made to order.

Indeed, although Louis Vuitton purses are known for being the target of counterfeiting, they remain widely popular in part due to their aura of authenticity, an aura that is bestowed by its leather material. In contrast, Prada purses made of nylon fibers lost popularity since nylon is an artificial material. In this case, the material decreased the aura of authenticity. Sunnie Wu received fake bags as gifts from friends and family. As she explained: "I care more about the benevolence I received from friends or family than whether it is real or fake." In this category of consumers, both counterfeit goods and brand name goods share a "gift" culture—they are souvenirs and gifts to maintain social relations.

A number of consumers that I interviewed associated their experiences buying counterfeit goods with feelings of embarrassment and shame. Yuling Tsai, a 45-year-old woman from Taiwan, married a Taiwanese immigrant who is a naturalized American citizen. She acquired her brand knowledge and wealth from her business in Libya during the period when the United States sanctioned Libya. She routinely buys luxury brand perfume and goods for her relatives. Yuling maintained that she never bought counterfeit products, but she once received a Chanel purse from a friend as a birthday gift. After a few months, Yuling found that the zipper was defective and brought it back to a Chanel store for repair with the original authenticity card, dust bag and gift box. The Chanel clerk took a quick glance at her purse and returned it, explaining: "We cannot fix it. This is a fake." Yuling told me: "I felt so ashamed and terrified, and I complained to the friend so that she would not make me lose face in front of the staff in Chanel again."

Other people experienced embarrassment not because they possessed a knockoff of a brand name, but because they possessed a product that *appeared* to be brand name. And it was the brand name product, and its aura of high social status and luxury consumption, that was embarrassing. Yiling Fang, for example, used to have a fake Burberry wallet, a gift from her younger sister's friend, which earned her the envy and attention of other girls. Yiling said: "That was when I began to learn about the interaction between brands and social class and people's interpretations of brand names." Two other informants I encountered in Xiangyang Market cited the intellectual property rights law as the reason not to purchase any fake products.

For some consumers, mixing and matching counterfeit goods with genuine brand name goods to deceive people was fun. Bowen He worked as a flight attendant for a Taiwanese airline company for six years. She went to shop for counterfeit accessories after hearing two other crewmembers' conversation about fake Louis Vuitton bags. According to the advice she received from the more experienced crew members, "small size fakes look more real." Bowen contended: "For a large size bag, one should get a real brand name—even if the rest you carry are fake products, other people would still think that they are real."

Juoqin Wang and her uncle suggested that counterfeit markets in Shenzhen served as a good market research site to observe trends in consumer goods as well as consumer behavior. As she explained: "China has become the index nation for marketing. Whatever releases in China will attract the attention of business people from other places. For instance, I would not be ashamed to buy a fake iPhone so that I can do research on it and show it off to my friends from the United States." To most consumers, consuming counterfeit goods produced positive experiences and emotions. Shujuan Xu enjoys "speed shopping" for counterfeit goods at sidewalk stands, and Jiyu Zhou described shopping for fakes as a "thrilling experience" simply because it gives her the feeling that she can afford brand name items.

As we can see, fake products are appropriated as tentative signs of social distinction. This may provide consumers a sense of satisfaction at having "deceived" others into thinking they are of a higher social status than they really are, or it may arouse in them a sense of embarrassment that they are now associated with such high status. Counterfeit goods are mass produced to supply lower class consumers. But, the knowledge of luxury goods increases the referential value of both the counterfeit good and the brand name. The story of Junda Yao illustrates the intricate relationship between fake and luxury goods. Yao spent six years selling fake products to cultivate his knowledge of luxury goods. He went on to spend eight years working as a salesman in a brand name boutique shop in order to make connections with celebrities, rich housewives and the daughters of rich businessmen. He eventually opened his own chain of 13 second-hand boutique stores in Hong Kong, Taipei, Beijing, and Macao. The functionality of consumer goods is almost always emphasized by consumers, due in part to the fact that these consumers are from lower income groups. Both counterfeit goods and brand name goods have aroused new trends in consumerism.

Class Exercise

1. Horace Chang was contracted by New Balance to make and distribute sneakers until New Balance canceled his contract. Horace Chang continued making shoes that bore the New Balance trademark without permission (Schmidle 2010). If you were the lawyer representing New Balance, what measures and steps would you take to stop the production of sneakers by Horace Chang?

5

COUNTERFEIT CULTURE AS PROTEST AND REBELLION

On November 12, 2008, some 100,000 copies of a fake July 4, 2009 edition of *The New York Times* were distributed around the corner of New York's Time Square and a couple of other locations. The front page featured the headlines of *Iraq War Ends* and *Nationalized Oil to Fund Climate Change Efforts* complemented by a fake Monsanto advertisement which said: "Ladybugs for pest control: A ladybug can eat up to 50 pests every day, without harming plants—making this little insect as effective as any pesticide. Now shipping to all farmers." The front page contained a spoofed motto: "All the news we hope to print," and it was revealed later that Bertha Suttners and the Yes Men group claimed partial responsibility for this prank. Two university professors, Jacque Servin and Igor Vamos, wearing aprons which said *New York Times*, actually led a group of cameramen to the front door of the real *New York Times* and confronted the security guards about their fake identities. In the movie *Yes Men Fix the World* (2009), Jacque Servin and Igor Vamos, who wrote, produced, and directed the movie, further explained the reason to organize this action: "We need a really ambitious plan to show how real change will look . . . (we need to be) back on track of how it was before things fell apart and set our imagination free." Later, they accepted interviews by the real journalists of CNBC, stating "We are trying to show how the world can be different." Several European television stations reported on this event in the news. The readers of the fake newspapers were not angry at the producers; instead, some said: "It's a dream newspaper, you wake up and all you want has come true."

The faux *New York Times* was only the latest of a series of activist plots hatched by the Yes Men. These included the "Barbie Liberation Organization," in which they purchased talking Barbie Dolls and GI Joes, altered the voice mechanisms to have Barbie exclaim "Vengeance is mine!" and GI Joes "Let's plan our dream wedding!" The altered dolls were surreptitiously placed back on store shelves with stickers saying "Call your local TV Station," to ensure media coverage and expose the hypocrisy of gender stereotyping. They went on to create fake websites such as dowethics.com to focus attention on the failure of Dow Chemical to fairly compensate victims of the explosion of the Union Carbide (which merged with Dow in 2001) chemical plant in Bhopal, India in 1984.

The Yes Men were following in the tradition of using counterfeit goods, web-sites, and identities (the Yes Men refer to themselves as "identity correctors") to protest corporate and government wrongdoing. Adbusters, one of the pioneers of what has become known as "culture jamming," produces spoof advertisements (see Figure 5.1) to protest the misleading claims of advertisers.

These actions illustrate how counterfeiting has been used, not only as an economic tool, but as a political device to protest and resist the abuse of corporate and government power. In China, also, we also see how culture jamming has been used as a "weapon of the weak" (Scott 1985).

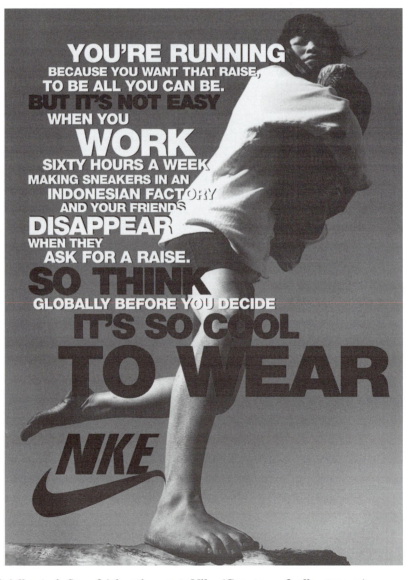

Figure 5.1 Adbuster's Spoof Advertisement: Nike (Courtesy of adbuster.org).

Only 44 days after the Yes Men distributed their fake *New York Times*, at the other end of the world in downtown Shenzhen, four *faux amis* of television journalists interviewed pedestrians on how they planned to spend their Christmas' Eve. Holding a plunger, a cooler fan base, and a bamboo clothes hanger for a camera tripod and a home video camera, the four young recent immigrant girls, who occupied white-collar or blue-collar day-jobs, called themselves the improvised "Fake Chinese Central Television journalists." Various Chinese newspapers released the photographs of this event and although the coverage focused on the appearances of these young "journalists" (including comments such as "they are no less pretty than the 'real television journalists'"), no media revealed the identities of them.

It appears that these events, from the fake distribution of the *New York Times* to fake interviews on Chinese Central Television News are similar yet different: the mockery's targets are both the elite journalism institutions of the two nations; as we "peel away the layers of onions" of the two events, they represent different types of culture jamming and resistance that are both local and global.

The glow of fireworks up in the sky, the parade of the lion and dragon, the red envelopes given by the elders and the televised Chinese Gala program form the collective experience of Chinese New Year at home or abroad. To be sure, these traditions are not so "traditional." They have undergone profound change as China's economy has expanded and changed. As such, they are more likely to be the experiences of China's younger generations; even for this generation, the ritual of watching the Spring Festival Gala on the lunar New Year's Eve on the state-run Chinese Central Television Company (CCTV) has itself been reinvented by a burgeoning copycat culture in China. Against the backdrop of a media-savvy counter-cultural movement, the Gala has been parodied and copied by artists and freethinkers and offered up to mass audiences as a cultural critique and alternative. These copycat galas give us a glimpse of what counterfeiting means in contemporary China and the culture that supports counterfeiting.

Mengqi Shi and Zehong He directed the first *Shanzhai* (copycat) Gala in late 2008, claiming that the program represented the grassroots spirit of the Chinese people. Shi grew up the son of peasants in Sichuan province and became a migrant worker and, later, a wedding planner in Beijing. He was well-versed in creative copycatting. "When I was a little boy," he explained, "I wanted so badly to drive a car, but then it was rare even to see a car on the road, let alone drive one. So I would make a car from blankets and drive in bed." Shi joined forces with Zehong He to set up a company and crew team to organize a *Shanzhai* gala. The copycat gala was scheduled to broadcast live on the Guizhou television station, a government-owned regional channel, but the station backed off at the last minute. Shi and He received a warning from the government that they lacked "performance approval" from the state to host the gala. In the end, the copycat gala was broadcast on the internet and on television by the Macao Satellite television station.

The first *Shanzhai* Gala was similar to the official CCTV Gala, except that all the performers were amateur and were voted on by internet users. The internet broadcast was criticized for its slow speed, but this was only because the viewership was so large it exceeded the capacity of the website. Though the program was also criticized for being unprofessional, foreign media like the *Wall Street Journal* were compelled to report on the story:

> The ebullient Mr. Shi sports close-cropped hair and collared-shirt-and-sweater combinations more suited to an office worker than a guerrilla filmmaker . . . in addition to the singing, dancing and comedy routines that populate the official CCTV gala, Mr. Shi's show will feature elements that even he finds difficult to categorize . . . performers include a pair of wheelchair acrobats and a singing five-year-old boy in an Elvis-style jumpsuit and pink wig. "I guess you could call these 'folk performances,' " he says.
>
> (Canaves and Ye 2009)

At the conclusion of the 2009 gala, Shi was broke. But the *Shanzhai* Gala had become a cultural icon. Exam questions on the gala appeared in a middle high school in Beijing and the entrance exam for Zhongnan University of Economics and Law. In 2010, Shi hosted another copycat gala and his efforts have sparked an entire genre of internet-based copycat galas, including the Northern Migrant Workers' Gala, the Civic Gala, the Farmers' Gala, the Gala of Chinese Studies, the Old Men's Gala, and the Southerner's Gala.[1]

Gala participants and viewers are diverse, ranging from college students to migrant workers. Taken as a whole, the galas have drawn viewers away from the state-sanctioned CCTV Gala, though this varies by region. As communications scholar Cheng-Liang Lee has indicated, the highest viewing rate for the CCTV Gala of 2009 was 89 percent in the Liaoning Province of Northeast China; the lowest viewing rate was 5 percent in the Guangdong Province of the Pearl River Delta (Lee 2009: 49). According to some estimates, there are one to three viewers of copycat galas for every six viewers of the CCTV Gala.

The director of the 2010 Northern Migrant Workers' Gala, Wenjun Shi, has said that "the first copycat gala helped the public realize that there's the way to make an active cultural choice. It is a festival for the people." Shi's Northern Migrant Workers' Gala emphasizes the bittersweet life of migrant workers in Beijing. The program editors visit several communities in Zhongguancun, Xidan, and 798 Art Zone to talk with migrant workers and to distribute free tickets to the gala (Wu 2010). This gala and others have attracted a large cross-section of China's workers and youth. "I used to spend New Year's Eve sitting around the dinner table with family members and watching the [CCTV] Gala," explained a migrant worker in Shanghai. "I couldn't go home this year, so I figured that I would watch the copycat gala with other internet users. It feels more in fashion to me. Internet copycat galas give us new 'taste' for television galas" (Li 2010). The majority of viewers of copycat galas were born after the 1980s.

This copycat culture has extended far beyond the Chinese New Year Gala. A *Shanzhai* version of a popular television education program called "Lecture Room" was broadcast on YouTube by a college graduate, Jianxue Han. Han's application to be on the actual program was rejected, so he developed his own version, using the internet as his broadcast medium. Later, college freshman Fangzhou Jiang imitated Han and broadcast her own commentaries on literature through the internet. In these cases, a kind of popular grassroots scholarship has arisen. Though these scholars are not recognized by formal academic institutions, they have cultivated a viewership and build a popular program using an existing show's program as their framework. Other cases of copycat practices include fake popular idols, with mainland-born persons acting in advertisements or television shows as stand-ins for celebrities like Jay Chou and "F4."

The Sincerest Form of Rebellion

Some argue that *shanzhai* culture represents popular innovations and a new wave of democracy. Xueran Xia, a sociologist at Beijing University, explains that "[*Shanzhai*] shows that the people need more channels to express themselves when they are not recognized by the mainstream culture. It will be more and more common." Xia points out that the internet supports the rise of this *shanzhai* culture. In contrast, another scholar at Beijing University, Yiwu Zhang, criticizes *shanzhai* galas, arguing that there is a threshold for professional artistic expression. Simply put, no other gala could outperform the CCTV Gala.

Chinese Youth Daily conducted a poll of 2,169 Chinese citizens on their views of *shanzhai* culture. The results showed that 57 percent of the people interviewed believed that *shanzhai* should not be regulated and free to air. Nineteen percent believed that *shanzhai* should be regulated and managed by the state. The rest had no comment. The poll also showed that the most-voted core values of the "*shanzhai* culture included: innovation (41 percent) and ambition (29 percent). Forty percent contended that *shanzhai* was a Do It Yourself (DIY) culture; 34 percent a copycat culture; and 34 percent a counterfeit culture. A full 30 percent of those interviewed believed that *shanzhai* culture was a form of stealing.

Literature critic, Xizhang Xie, suggests that when the traditional CCTV Gala became less popular, the *shanzhai* version sprang up naturally to attract people for its variety and newness. "Despite its coarse techniques and operation, *shanzhai* culture meets the psychological demands of common people and could be a comfort to their minds," said he explained (China Daily 2008). The Director-General of the Beijing Municipal Cultural Bureau, Gongming Jiang said that as long as *shanzhai* culture is enjoyed by the common people and as long as it is "healthy," it will be supported by the municipal authority (Minyingjingjibao 2010). Binjie Liu from the National Copyright Administration of PRC claimed that "*shanzhai* shows the cultural creativity of the common people. It fits a market need, and people like it. We have to guide *shanzhai* culture and regulate it" (Schmidle 2010).

Although *shanzhai* culture is a copycat culture, it may also be read as a grass-roots subculture. In this case, imitation has become the sincerest form of rebellion. Indeed, *shanzhai* culture has inherited the spirit of the culture jamming. In the 2001 movie *Culture Jam: Hijacking Commercial Culture*, culture jamming is defined as "the right to reconfigure the logo, to steal other people's ideas, remaking them into your own, and go out and do something new."

However popular, commodification and censorship are major issues for the *shanzhai* galas as they are for *shanzhai* culture as a whole. Some cultural critics worry that the copycat galas have been turned into a commercial show, rather than a movement that represents grassroots culture (Wu 2010). Once popular culture is commoditized, however, its potential to be a liberating form of expression is lost. Censorship by the state department of culture is another concern. The CCTV Gala was seen as an important ritual to display the state authority over its people, with recurring themes of national prosperity and patriotism (Jinwanbao 2010). *Shanzhai* galas threaten the state's control over cultural content and distract viewers from this core expression of state control in China. As for the CCTV Gala, it has reacted to the copycat gala movement by changing its 2010 Gala to be an interactive, online program. Through the internet, it has allowed the audience to vote from a wish-list of performers during the year before the performance. In doing so, it successfully offset the criticism that it was a top-down model of production.

State control of cultural content hinges on its control over television. Likewise, the culturally rebellious thread in China's copycat culture rests on innovative use of new technology, such as the internet. Of the two media, television is the more popular. There are more television stations in China than any other country in the world: approximately 2,646 stations in 2009, up from 12 stations in 1965. The Chinese television viewing audience reached 1.2 billion in 2007 and television remains the most popular medium in China. Just under 100 percent of Chinese households have television sets, and 94 percent of Chinese people regard watching television as the most important entertainment during their leisure time. On average, a Chinese person watches more than three hours of television per day (Liu, Liu, Xu and Zhang 2008).

Television programming is organized at four administrative levels—national (CCTV), provincial, city, and county. Australian researcher Michael Keane has observed that China's massive television infrastructure is:

> a legacy of decades of state control over media industries by which cultural bureaucrats exercised surveillance over form and content. It is also a legacy of a system that has tied production units to their respective parent broad-caster, obliging the unit to produce for that stations' viewers. The effect has been a stagnant and carnivorous production environment, devoid of any real innovation . . . everyone rushes in and produces the same kinds of products and targets the same markets within a particular locality.
>
> (Keane 2002)

In contrast, access to the internet is more limited and currently Chinese citizens are struggling against the state's active controlling, monitoring and censoring of the internet. The Chinese state has tightened its control not only over the internet, but over text messages on cell phones. This has the convenient effect of stifling political demonstrations. In January of 2010, a sophisticated hacking attack targeted Google email users, most of them human rights activists. In response, Google Inc. threatened to shut down its operation in China. Many internet users left bouquets outside the entrance of Google Inc.'s office. In the end, the sustainability of China's copycat culture depends on the government's willingness to foster multiculturalism.

Class Exercise

1. Do you know any case of copy culture which rebels against the mainstream culture from your own culture or your own town? Please illustrate the origin of the case and its consequences.

6

CONCLUSION

Over a 20-year period, China has become the world's third-largest economy and has formed a culture of self-interest, rank materialism, and growing cynicism. The study of counterfeiting captures China's unique "post-development state," in the words of the *shanzhai* Godfather, Ming-Kai Tsai. As opposed to the modern paradigm, the copy culture in China has come to reflect a post-modern parody of present-day capitalist societies. Consumerism and culture do not sit opposite one another at two ends of a spectrum, as Igor Kopytoff suggested. Rather, gray zones of new meanings circulate among fake producers and counterfeit consumers, which counter traditional binary oppositions between high and low, material and cultural, fake and real, and legal and extralegal.

My examination of the counterfeiting trade contributes to a deeper understanding of not simply China, but the cultural politics of intellectual property rights and consumption in the globalization era. Walter Benjamin and Rosemary Coombe remind us that during an age of simulated reality, the technical evolution from mechanical to electronic reproductions of images made the world a place that values copies and simulations over the originals. As Coombe suggests:

> What is quintessentially human is the capacity to make meanings, challenge meanings, and transform meanings . . . Humanity is stripped through overzealous application and continuous expansion of intellectual property rights protections. With no reductionist intention to see the power of intellectual property rights in purely prohibitory terms, legal enforcement of copyright, publicity, and trademark rights, however, may create danger for democratic dialogue, which includes ongoing negotiation and struggle over meaning as an essential part.
>
> Coombe (2005: 122)

If we examine closely the mechanisms surrounding the world of brand names, we find that it is the trademark, the image rather than the actual quality of material or precision of work that generates a product's added value. This explains why corporations spend huge amounts of money on the prevention of trademark piracy and litigation over trademark and copyright violations.

Rosemary Coombe (2005) has called attention to the power relationship that exists between the owners of intellectual property and everyone else, in particular the unorthodox use of manufactured signs in popular culture. The invention of intellectual property rights law in the West makes many once non-material "things" into property-objects. By objectifying and reifying cultural forms, intellectual property rights laws freeze the meanings of cultural symbols and fence off fields of cultural meanings. The right to control a trademark and thus to fix the signifier symbol's meaning is potentially perpetual, as are the rights to patent, publicity and copy.[1] The result is that in North American society "owners" of trademarks became the most powerful and wealthy actors. "The more valuable the mark becomes, the more legal protection it receives, which of course means that it accrues even more value because it is granted further immunity from scrutiny, competition, or denigration" (Coombe 2005: 119).

One case from Taiwan is telling in this regard. A company from Taiwan, Foxconn China, hired more than 1,000 lawyers to ensure the protection of its connector products.[2] Employees of Foxconn referred to this strategy as a "patent mine", since any competitor in the connector sector could easily "trigger" a violation and lawsuit. The strategy successfully intimidated Foxconn's competitors and maintained Foxconn's status as the world's top company in connector manufacture. Moreover, the enactment of trademark law has endorsed and sanctioned brand name fetishism in modern society. In response, the *shanzhai* economy and culture in China has emerged as a transnational subculture that supplies rebellious resistance to brand name fetishism by less powerful social actors.

Farmers of a village in Jiangsu Province, now known as "the wealthiest village in China," built a fake U.S. Capitol next to an "Arc de Triomphe," a Gate of Heavenly Peace, and a mini Great Wall. That version of the U.S. Capitol even has the Statue of Liberty transplanted on top of it—two famous sights rolled into one. A district in Beijing City and Chongqing City in Sichuan Province have created similar replications to attract tourists and to house government offices. There are hundreds of other copycat structures sprinkled throughout China. In Chongqing Municipality in Southwest China, a salon owner built a *shanzhai* version of the famous "Water Cube" Olympic venue in Beijing. In Nanjing, a new shopping mall has a McDonald's look-alike burger bar called "OMC McDnoald's," a Starbucks-style coffee shop called "Bucksstar Coffee," and an imitation Pizza Hut called "Pizza Huh." City bosses are under pressure to ban the shops after pictures of the fake stores were leaked. Finally, a section of Erhuan North Road of Chengdu, Sichuan has 43 fake brand name shops ranging from the shoe store "Odidos" to a Chinese-style pork and rice restaurant advertising McDonald's trademark. "These trademarks catch people's eye balls," stated one shop owner (Huang and Guo 2009).

There is another trend of copying in Chinese architectural design. As Chinese scholar Danqing Chen writes:

> The urban landscapes that we live in today in China are the remediated, faked, simulated, fantasized, hurriedly built and inappropriately luxurious and exaggerative versions of "Hong Kong," "Europe," or "Manhattan." It is like a migrant worker who wears a Western suit and a tie, who is a mimicry of the first person who wears a Western suit and a tie instead of a real Hong Kongese or Westerner.[3]

(Chen 2008)

Indeed, during urban development of China's post–Economic Transformation Period, Chinese real estate developers not only built up a mall of fake brands but also promoted residential buildings ornamented with Greek pillars and statues of the goddess Venus. More recently, lifestyles and architectural styles merging Chinese and Western culture are being promoted by developers. The buildings appear European on the outside, but inside they contain traditional Chinese style gardens, which resemble the mystified Royal Yuanming Garden (burnt down by the Western troops during the war of 1899). In this instance, collective social memory and cultural identities linked to public space are transformed by global capitalism.

Figure 6.1 **The "American Capitol Hill" in China.**

Figure 6.2 **Bird's-Eye View of the village in Figure 6.1.**

Figure 6.3 **The Shanzhai Cinderella Castle of Shijingshan Amusement Park.**

Besides Huaxi Village, there is the state-run *Shijingshan* Amusement Park in Beijing, which provides the most extreme case of *shanzhai* culture. At the park, Disney characters like Mickey Mouse and Donald Duck walked around with Doraemon and Hello Kitty, two famous Japanese animation characters, charging RMB 5 for a photo. The rides and attractions in the Park include rides identical to those found at Disneyland, such as the Pirate Ship and Cinderella Castle. But the park had neither required nor acquired permission to use the characters, logos and images from Disney Time Warner Company. Each year,

Figure 6.4 **The "Fantastically European Street Shop" of Shijingshan Amusement Park.**

1.5 million visitors go to the park, resulting in an annual revenue of RMB 15 million. The Chinese president of *Shijingshan* defended the park's use of Disney characters with the following statement: "[Mickey Mouse] is actually a cat with two big ears." The official website of the park was once shut down after being reported by foreign media. As of May 2010, however, the unauthorized characters were gone. Pirate ship and Cinderella castle remained popular spots.

Is copycatting an integral part of Chinese culture? In an article entitled "The Cultural Origin of Chinese Counterfeit Products" published by the Voice of Germany (Deutsche Welle), the Secretary-General of the Germany–China Economic Association provides a cultural explanation Chinese counterfeiting. He claims that because traditional Chinese Confucian education requires reciting and copying, students essentially learn to copy. A similar argument was made about Japanese culture, though Japan has now matched the success of the United

States, Germany and Italy by adding Tokyo to the elite cluster of world-class industrial design and fashion cities. Antonia Finnane (2008) argues that drive for mass production and the contested and suppressed politics in China have inhibited an independent and innovative fashion industry in China. And yet, when we look at the *shanzhai* phenomena, we find that counterfeiters have developed their own brands, catered to local tastes, and innovated designs in spite of the fact that they are essentially copying others. They have also honed "fast-fashion" and "open system" concepts by catering to markets that are underserved by brand name manufacturers. For these reasons, Ming-Kai Tsai has argued that *shanzhai* should be defined as a legal, "disruptive innovation" business model.[4]

Arjun Appadurai argues that exclusivity, followed by authenticity, plays an important role in determining a commodity's value. These concerns for exclusivity and authenticity revolve around discourses of good taste, expert knowledge, design innovation, and social distinction, which are all particularly acute in the world of art and fashion. But who says that art and fashion must begin with originality? Likewise, who says that art and fashion has ever begun with originality? As Walter Benjamin reminds us:

> Until the nineteenth century, the copy of an original work had its own value, it was a legitimate practice. In our own time the copy is illegitimate, inauthentic: it is no longer "art." Similarly, the concept of forgery has changed—or rather, it suddenly appears with the advent of modernity.[5]
>
> (Benjamin (1968[1936]: 103)

Returning to Takashi Murakami's exhibition, in which Louis Vuitton bags were displayed as if on display in a Chinatown market, the boundary between commodity and art is often blurred. Here, the *shanzhai* culture of China is reproduced in the "original, art world" based in New York or Beijing, both powerful urban repositories of culture. High society is first celebrated and copied by *shanzhai* culture, then examined and mocked by *shanzhai* culture. Likewise, *shanzhai* culture is first denigrated by high society, then embraced as real, even fashionable cultural expression. Counterfeiters are not simply aping high society; they have become producers of meaning and cultural innovators. Perhaps human culture has always been characterized by an endless series of imitations.

Class Exercise

1. Please create your own artwork or project of copy culture, which is culturally rebellious and demonstrate to your classmates the idea and messages behind your presentation. The format could be a drawing, PowerPoint slides, a song, a movie; you could employ other multimedia tools for your project.

NOTES

1 INTRODUCTION

1 In the spring of 2010, I attended a gallery reception for a flowery and vibrant Chinese Ink and Wash Painting exhibition. The artist was Hsiao-Jung Ni, an established Chinese artist and my university colleague. At the exhibition, both the real Chinese brush paintings in color and mechanical prints were on display, and I overheard guests' conversations about how surprising it was that the reproductions are conforming to reality. Ni taught me and other guests to look closely at the details of the brushes and inks of the painting; one could still see the layer of ink of the real to tell from the reproduction. However, Ni also noted that even connoisseurs' eyes could be fooled when the ink layer is very thin, and one has to rely on the creditability of the artist and facilitation of modern technology for ultimate authentication. Depending on the choice of artistic presentation and proportion of water in the ink, the ink layer can be so thin on the paper and one cannot tell by eye. Hence, it is very hard to tell the real from the fakes.

2 For more exhibition information, see http://www.brooklynmuseum.org/exhibitions/murakami/

3 *Bangmingpai* is another popular term in Shanghai referring to counterfeit goods. *Bang* literally means "next to," and *mingpai* means "brand names." The term implies an intention on the part of the counterfeiter to "get close to the brand name" by using similar or exact logos of brand names in order to misguide consumers into believing that these goods have connections with the real brand name owners.

4 Consumerism refers to a condition against the backdrop of economic boom in the 1950s United States when people had gained increasing purchasing power to produce and purchase a range of products beyond the bare necessities. Aided by an advertising industry skilled in developing a range of ways to convince people to purchase more and more, Americans purchased televisions, automobiles, homes, and clothes in record numbers. As Eisend and Schucher-Güler (2006) note, the willingness of consumers to purchase a counterfeit product seems to increase if they can rate the quality of a product before purchase and to decrease if they cannot. The new Marxist school sees branding, advertising, personal selling, packaging display, and design as actions that create symbolic meanings for commodities and tempt consumers by promising them an enhanced identity.

5 See the website of WTO: http://www.wto.org/english/tratop_e/trips_e/intel1_e.htm

6 However, under some circumstances, a compulsory license will be granted to restrict this exclusive power.

7 Some of the forgo studies on China in relation to intellectual property rights emphasized on the explanation of cultural tradition, such as the emphasis on memorizing literature word by word in traditional education. Others traced back the emphasis of good forgery as a criterion for good calligraphy to the Six Dynasties to explain why modern Chinese infringes intellectual property rights. The debate about ensuring intellectual property rights dates back to the middle of the 19th century, when the Taiping Rebellion came up with one initiative to draft a patent law to encourage Chinese innovation (Schmidle 2010).

Japan used to be the finger-pointing counterfeiter immediately after WWII, but then Japanese companies became respectful competitors.

8   Through importation and reimportation, fake drugs enter into country supplies and end up in drug stores, and, ultimately, in patients who ingest or are injected with them. See Liang, Bryan A. 2006. "Fade to Black: Importation and Counterfeit Drugs." *American Journal of Law and Medicine, 32*, pp. 279.

9   Commodity theory provides a framework for an investigation of the relationship between scarcity and value perception and for answering the question of whether and how the loss of the exclusivity of a brand induces a decrease in consumer demand for counterfeit versions. Furthermore, the willingness of consumers to purchase a counterfeit product seems to increase if they can rate the quality of a product before purchase and to decrease if they cannot (Eisend and Schucher-Güler 2006).

10 The International Anti-Counterfeiting Coalition (IACC) is the world's largest non-government organization or interest group, which advocates for protecting intellectual property and deterring counterfeiting. Its membership spans from automotive, apparel, luxury goods, and pharmaceuticals, to food, software, and entertainment. Based in the United States, IACC has hosted annual conferences for two decades, which provides a venue for discussions about enforcement issues in different countries for the brand name owners and attorneys. In Taiwan, there are several active interest groups which have monitored the counterfeiting activities. For instance, the International Federation of the Phonographic Industry was founded in 1986 to protect the copyright of the music industry. Business Software Alliance (founded in 1988), Foundation for the Protection of Film and Video Works Affiliate of Motion Picture Association (MPA), and other local interest groups also constantly report leads to the police to conduct investigations.

11 In a survey conducted in 2006, two-thirds of Britons say that they are happy to own fake clothing, footwear, watches and other items. Favorite brands for fakers remain Louis Vuitton, Gucci and Burberry. In a 2008 BBC survey, 24 percent of Britons have bought counterfeit fashion goods such as sunglasses or handbags. In June 2010, the BBC disclosed another survey result that nearly a quarter of UK consumers say they would buy fake World Cup branded goods to save money. It says counterfeiting of South Africa 2010 products is rife, with about a fifth of goods likely to be fakes, losing legitimate businesses $72 million.

12 A branch of the China Small Commodities City market of Yiwu located in Wulumuqui in Xinjiang Province serves as an export post for the Middle East and Eastern Europe.

13 Several reasons contribute to this phenomenon. New York's port has 13.4 percent of total U.S. container traffic. New York City's per capita income is 22 percent higher than the U.S. average. New York City's high sales tax creates further demand for untaxed, low-priced counterfeit goods. Finally, the city has the largest U.S. urban population and hosts significant numbers of visitors that generate high demand for both legal and counterfeit goods (Thompson 2004: 1).

2   THE STRUCTURE OF A COUNTERFEIT INDUSTRY

1   This chip invention is termed "turn key" by the cell phone industry since the hardware and software for cell phones were packaged into a single chip. Turn key solutions were previously available only to small and medium mobile phone suppliers that developed them without a license. However, they have recently entered the production lines of mainstream cell phone manufacturers. This development is expected to help bolster China's standing in the world market as a developer and producer of quality cell phones (Global Sources 2009).

2   CRT stands for Cathode Ray Tube, which is a vacuum tube containing an electron gun (a source of electrons) and a fluorescent screen; LCD stands for liquid crystal display which is a thin, flat electronic visual display that uses the light modulating properties of liquid crystals.

3 Previously, New Delhi rebuffed an attempt to bring cheap laptops to India through the U.S.-led One Laptop Per Child program.

3 THE MARKET OF COUNTERFEIT GOODS

1 The last emperor of China, Aixinjueluo Puyi, who was forced to remove his imperial gown, wore Western-style clothes. He also wore sunglasses and used a walking stick, the style of a "British gentleman" at the time.
2 Xiangyang Bian, a professor from China, talked at China Study Group, Fairbank Center, 1730 Cambridge Street, CGIS S050 Harvard University, February 28, 2007.
3 Dr. Sun Yat-Sen served as President and Temporary President for several different terms in the Republic of China.
4 In old urban districts and in the countryside "long-robe horse-gowns"—a ceremonial, wide-sleeved jacket of a Mandarin—remained fashionable, despite waves of revolution and criticism from the communist government.
5 Coming of age ceremonies exist in many societies in the form of legal convention or as part of a ritualistic cycle, or *rite de passage* to mark the transition point when a young person becomes an adult (Keesing 1986: 850). The Chinese coming of age ceremony was practiced under the rule of the Duke of Chou (1100 B.C.) until 1911. For men, age 20 was called *Guan Li*, and for women it was called *Ji Li*. These ceremonies are rarely practiced in post-Revolution China. In Japan, coming of age ceremonies, or *seijin shiki*, are still held in government buildings on the second Monday of January annually. Girls wear kimono to attend the ceremony.

4 CONSUMING COUNTERFEIT GOODS

1 In response, the Ministry of Economic Development of Italy created the Department of the Fight Against Counterfeiting and abolished the post of high commissioner for the fight against counterfeiting in 2009. On April 21, 2010 a 24-year-old woman was charged for illegally bypassing the copyright of the product label, together with the merchant. She was fined €200 ($162) and the bag was confiscated. The buyer was the first victim consumer being fined for purchasing counterfeit within Italy and charged against *Law 99*. The Italian police now regularly check posts in local markets of small cities and suburbs. This case shows a turning point that a client of a counterfeiter is now seen as a conspirator of street peddlers. It is estimated by Italian media that in 2009 alone, the police confiscated a total of 7,000 pairs of counterfeit shoes, 1.7 million counterfeit cigarettes, 900,000 fake Disney toys, and 700,000 pirated Microsoft software. According to *Polizia Municipale* in the first four months of 2010, 42 million fake products were confiscated, outnumbering a total number of 40 million fake goods in 2009 by 2 million. Drastic measures are reasoned to be taken in Jesolo of Venice Municipality, Forte dei Marmi of Lucca Municipality, Castiglione della Pescaia, and the shores of Genova and Rome. In Forte dei Marmi, the bylaw literally banishes peddlers on the beaches, where policemen keep watch on vehicles regularly. In Castiglione della Pescaia, only the licensed 25 peddlers are allowed to sell their handcrafts on the beaches of the town, wearing yellow caps and T-shirts to distinguish from the rest. In Genova and Rome, the locals reported that more checkpoints have been set up and closed surveillance has been conducted by the police to watch for counterfeit trade. In Jesolo, a regulation promulgated by the Major Francesco Calzavara is said to have transformed "its beach into a militarized, heavily monitored zone" in June 2010. At less than every 1 kilometer, there is a baywatcher's viewpoint for counterfeit trade. A retired 65-year-old Australian lady named Ursula Corel was penalized 1,000 Euro (US $1,254)for purchasing a US $7 fake purse from a *vu cumprà*, or African peddler on the beach of Jesolo. Ursula Corel told the Italian journalists that "this is an impossible sum to pay as I am only a retired woman." Ursula Corel is a victim of the anti-*vu cumprà*

campaign. Everyday, a binocular-equipped police force stands on the baywatch view-points to clear the fake trade from the city center and the beaches. In addition to that, 20 members of the police force have been deployed along the 15 kilometer coastline.

2 http://www.taobao.com/

3 The small commodity market consists of items such as toys, beads, and telescopes.

4 The Port of New York accounted for 13 percent of all containers imported to the United States in 2003 (Padavan 2005a).

5 These two forms of competition—vertical and horizontal—are related. A local government's ability to bargain for a higher degree of autonomy vis-à-vis central control will enhance its competitive edge against other regions. In the same vein, a locality that succeeds in outperforming other regions will increase its bargaining power vis-à-vis the central government.

6 Others disagree, pointing to the need for land as the major reason that the market was shut down.

7 Mertha (2005) has analyzed the role of the Administration of Industry and Commerce, the branch of local government responsible for regulating and policing commercial activity, in detail in Chapter 5 of *The Politics of Piracy*.

8 Pseudonym by the request of the officer.

9 In 2009, Taiwan was removed from the Special 301 list.

10 In 2010, an inter-ministry task team was set up in the Executive Yuan of Taiwan to prevent counterfeiting activities. The team includes members from the Bureau of Standards, Metrology and Inspection, Ministry of Economic Affairs, Intellectual Property Rights Office, local governments and Intellectual Property Rights Police. A toll-free phone number is available for reporting counterfeiting activities by any person or victims.

11 The grass-root, anti-counterfeiting campaigns in China have been controversial and dramatic, as represented by the "Wang Hai phenomenon." Dubbed the "anti-counterfeiting folk hero." and "the No. 1 anti-counterfeiter," Wang Hai is China's best-known consumer rights activist, famous for his use of China's *Consumer Rights and Interests Protection Law*. In 1993, China adopted the *Consumer Rights and Interests Protection Law*. As a scholar of Architecture, Winnie Wong (n.d.) has watched this Wang Hai phenomenon closely, and noted that Wang Hai learned of a little-known article in it that compensates any consumer who purchases a counterfeit or substandard product with a double refund from the vendor. Wang Hai first tested this law by purchasing 12 pairs of counterfeit Sony head-phones on sale at an electronics shop in a Beijing shopping mall. He then obtained double refund from the vendor after months of legal battles. Wang Hai's successful lawsuit, aided by one of the drafters of the law itself, inspired thousands of copycats throughout China.

12 In their multisited research (in the United States, Turkey, and Denmark) investigating the basis for passionate consumption and the roles of consumers, marketers and culture in the process, Belk, Ger and Askegaard (2003) classify the objects of desire in consumption into several types: "a quest for otherness," "sociality," "danger," and "inaccessibility."

13 Japanese anthropologist Koichi Iwabuchi and other scholars distinguish between Japanese "cute culture" and American "sexy culture." "Cute culture" refers to grownup obsessions with certain cartoon characters, popular culture, or clothing styles that would be considered incongruously juvenile or frivolous in other cultures. One example is the popularity of Hello Kitty characters among housewives and businesswomen.

5   COUNTERFEIT CULTURE AS PROTEST AND REBELLION

1 The official website of Shi's Copycat Gala is at http://www.ccstv.net

6   CONCLUSION

1 A similar point is raised in Laughlin's book *The Crime of Reason* (2008), Chapter 5: Patently Absurd.

2 A connector is a conductive device for joining electrical circuits together. Commonly used connectors include USB connectors or power connectors.
3 Author's translation.
4 Ming Kai Tsai's speech on *shanzhai* at National Tsing-Hwa University, Hsinchu Taiwan on April 20, 2009. (Broadcast on Udn.com.)
5 In *The Work of Art in the Age of Mechanical Reproduction*, Walter Benjamin recognized that the aura of the authentic work of art is tied up with its originality, and this aura is jeopardized by modern reproductive technologies.

BIBLIOGRAPHY

Adrian, Bonnie 2003 *Framing the Bride: Globalizing Beauty and Romance in Taiwan's Bridal Industry*. Berkeley: University of California Press.

Akhtar, Salman 2005 *Objects of Desire*. New York: Harmony Books.

Albers-Miller, Nancy D. 1999 Consumer misbehavior: why people buy illicit goods. *Journal of Consumer Marketing 16*(3): 273–287.

Alford, William 1995 *To Steal a Book is an Elegant Offense*. Stanford: Stanford University Press.

Anderson, Benedict 1991 *Imagined Communities*. London and New York: Verso.

Anderson, E. 1990 *The Food of China*. New Haven: Yale University Press.

Appadurai, Arjun 1986 Introduction: commodities and the politics of value. In *The Social Life of Things*. Arjun Appadurai ed. pp. 3–63. London: Cambridge University Press.

—— 1996 *Modernity at Large*. Minneapolis: University of Minnesota Press.

Ashkenazi, Michael, and John Clammer 2000 *Consumption and Material Culture in Contemporary Japan*. London and New York: Kegan Paul International.

Asia Times Online 2006 *Shanghai Now the World's Largest Cargo Port*. January 7.

Bakhtin, Mikhail 1968 *Rabelais and His World*. Cambridge, MA: MIT Press.

Barber, Benjamin 2007 *Consumed: How Markets Corrupt Children, Infantilize Adults, and Swallow Citizens Whole*. New York: W W Norton & Co Inc.

Barboza, D. 2010 China admits new tainted-milk case is older. *New York Times,* January 7.

Barthes, Roland 1985 *Fashion System*. London: Cape.

Barton, Antony 2007 Are fake goods a growing problem for procurement? *Supply Management 12*(2): 11.

Baudrillard, Jean 1998 *The Consumer Society: Myths and Structures*. London: Sage.

Beckor, G. S. 2008 *Report for Congress: Food and Agricultural Imports from China*. Congressional Research Service, September 26.

Belk, Russell with Güliz Ger and Søren Askegaard 2003 The fire of desire: A multisited inquiry into consumer passion. *Journal of Consumer Research 30*(3): 326–351.

Belk, Russell with Timothy Devinney and Giana Eckhardt 2005 Consumer Ethics Across Cultures. *Consumption, Markets & Culture 8*(3): 275–289.

Benjamin, Walter 1936 *The Work of Art in the Age of Mechanical Reproduction*. New York: Schoken Book.

Bergman, Justin 2010 Top ten Chinese knockoffs. *Time Magazine,* June 22.

Bestor, Theodore 2004 *Tsukiji*. Berkeley: University of California Press.

Bhabha, Homi 2004 *The Location of Culture*. London: New York: Routledge.

Bhagwati, Jaqdish 2004 *In Defense of Globalization*. New York: Oxford University Press.

Bian, Xiangyang 2007 "20th Century Chinese fashion." Talk delivered at China Study Group, Fairbank Center, 1730 Cambridge Street, CGIS S050 Harvard University, February 28 2007.

Biehl, João with Byron Good and Arthur Kleinman 2007 Introduction: Rethinking subjectivity. In *Subjectivity: Ethnographic Investigations*. João Biehl, Byron Good and Arthur Kleinman eds. pp. 1–23. Berkeley: University of California Press.

Boehm, Mike 2009 Louis Vuitton suit adds fraud allegation. *Los Angeles Times*, April 23.

Bourdieu, Pierre 1984 *Distinction: A Social Critique of the Judgment*. Cambridge: MA, Harvard University Press.

British Broadcast Corporation 2007 *UK Consumers Happy to Own Fakes*. July 23.

—— 2008 *Fifth of Britons "Buy Fake Goods."* February 15.

—— 2010 *World Cup: One in Four Would Buy Fake Goods*. June 9.

Brown, Dan 2003 *The Da Vinci Code*. New York: Doubleday.

Canaves, Yves and Juliet Ye 2009 Imitation is the sincerest form of rebellion in China. *Wall Street Journal*, January 22.

Chadha, Radha and Paul Husband 2007 *The Cult of the Luxury Brand: Inside Asia's Love Affair with Luxury*. Boston: Nicholas Brealey Publishing.

Chang, Chengan 2007 Meiguo minpai fangmaohuo wufenpu gongranmai jingfang chahuo shangwanjien. [Police Caught Sales of Counterfeits of American Brands in Wufengpu.] *ETToday News*, August 21.

Chang, Hsiao-hung 2004 Fake logos, fake theory, fake globalization. Trans. Yung-chao Liao. *Inter-Asia Cultural Studies* 5(2): 222–236.

Chen, Danqing 2008 *Tuebuji*. [*The Essays of Regression*]. Taipei: Lixu Publishing.

Chiang, Yi-chi 2008 Lupitaigu Shanzhai zhenhandan. [China Outside, Taiwan Inside Shanzhai Production.] *CW Magazine*, December 25.

Chi, Haifan 2009 *Sanxin tihejuo zhongguo shanzhaichang jujue*. [*Samsung's Proposal of Cooperation was Rejected by Shanzhai Workshops*] Seoul: Chosun Online, March 3.

China Daily 2008 *Copycat "Shanzhai" Culture Takes on Life of Its Own in China*, December 30.

Choi, E. Kwan 2006 *Mixed Markets with Counterfeit Producers*. Staff General Research Papers, Iowa State University, Department of Economics.

Choudhury, Santanu 2009 Tata hopes tiny car is a big hit. *Wall Street Journal*, March 21.

Chow, Daniel C. K. 2003 Organized crime, local protectionism, and the trade in counterfeit goods in China. *China Economic Review 14*: 473–484.

—— 2004 *Counterfeiting in China and is Effects on U.S. Manufacturing*. Written testimony.

Chua, Beng-Huat. 1998 World cities, globalization and the spread of consumerism: A view from Singapore. *Urban Studies* 35(5–6): 981–1000.

Clammer, John 2000 The global and the local: Gender, class, and the internationalization of consumption in a Tokyo neighborhood. In *Consumption and Material Culture in Contemporary Japan*. Michael Ashkenazi and John Clammer eds. pp. 249–283. London and New York: Kegan Paul International.

Coltman, Viccy 2001 Sir William's Hamilton's vase publications (1766–1776). *Journal of Design History 14*(1): 1–16.

Conley, Dalton 2001 Race, class, and eyes upon the street: Public space, social control and the economies of three urban communities. *Sociological Forum 16*(4): 759–772.

Coombe, Rosemary 2005 Objects of property and subjects of politics. In *Law and Anthropology: A Reader*. Sally Falk Moore ed. pp. 111–123. Malden: Blackwell Publishing.

Counihan, C. and P. Van Esterik eds. 1997 *Food and Culture: A Reader*. New York: Routledge.

Cox, Rupert 2007 *The Culture of Copying in Japan*. New York: Routledge.

Craik, Jennifer 1993 *The Face of Fashion: Cultural Studies in Fashion*. London: Routledge.

Davidson, Martin 1992 *The Consumerist Manifesto: Advertising in Postmodern Times*. London and New York: Routledge.

Derrida, Jacques 1992 *Given Time: I. Counterfeiting Money*. Chicago: University of Chicago Press.

Dimitrov, Martin 2004 *Administrative Decentralization, Legal Fragmentation, and the Rule of Law in Transitional Economies: The Enforcement of Intellectual Property Rights Law in China, Russia, Taiwan, and the Czech Republic*. Ph.D. dissertation, Department of Political Science, Stanford University.

Douglas, Mary and Baron Isherwood 1979 *The World of Goods: Towards an Anthropology of Consumption*. New York: Norton.

Duncombe, Stephen ed. 2002 *Culture Resistance Reader*. New York: Verso.

Duneier, Mitchell 1999 *Sidewalk*. New York: Farrar, Straus and Giroux.

Eco, Umberto 1998 *Faith in Fakes*. London: Vintage.

Economist 2007a *Briefing Italian Luxury Goods*. April 14: 75–76.

—— 2007b *Mind Games: Counterfeit Goods in China*. November 8: 82.

—— 2010 *Knock-offs Catch On*. March 6: 69–70.

Eisend M. and Schucher-Güler, P. 2006 Explaining counterfeit purchases: A review and pre-view. *Academy of Marketing Science Review* volume 2006(12) Available: http://www.amsreview.org/articles/eisend12-2006.pdf

Epstein, Gady 2009 Counterfeit cool. *Forbes Magazine*, February 16.

Evans-Pritchard, E. E. 1969 *The Nuer*. New York: Oxford University Press.

Ewen, Stuart 2001 *Captains of Consciousness: Advertising and the Social Roots of Consumer Culture*. New York: Basic Books.

Finnane, Antonia 2008 *Changing Clothes in China: Fashion, History, Nation*. New York: Columbia University Press.

Fiske, John 1989 *Understanding Popular Culture*. New York: Routledge.

Foster, Robert John 2008 *Coca-globalization: Following Soft Drinks from New York to New Guinea*. New York: Palgrave Macmillan

Foucault, Michel 1984 On the genealogy of ethics, In *The Foucault Reader*, Paul Rabinow ed. pp. 340–372, New York: Pantheon.

Galloni Alessandra 2007 Prada vs. Prada: Overcoming fashion phobia. *Wall Street Journal*, January 18: D1.

Gay, Paul du with Stuart Hall, Linda Janes, Hugh Mackay and Keith Negus 1997 *Doing Cultural Studies: The Story of the Sony Walkman*. London: Sage.

Geertz, Clifford 1973 *The Interpretation of Cultures*. New York: Basic Books.

Goody, Jack 2006 *The Theft of History*. Cambridge: Cambridge University Press.

Graeber, David 2002 The anthropology of globalization (with notes on Neomedievalism, and the End of the Chinese Model of the Nation-State). *American Anthropologist 104*(4): 1222–1227.

Grossman, G. 1986 *Counterfeit Product Trade*. C.E.P. R. Discussion Papers, CEPR: 103.

Grossman, Gene M. and Carl Shapiro 1988 Counterfeit-product trade. *The American Economic Review 78*(1): 59–75.

Ha, S., and S. Lennon 2006 Fashion intent for fashion counterfeit products: Ethical ideologies, ethical judgments, and perceived risks. In *Clothing and Textile Research Journal 24*(4), 297–315.

Hamilton, Gary 2006 *Commerce and Capitalism in Chinese Societies*. London and New York: Routledge.

Hannertz, Ulf 1996 *Transnational Connections*. New York: Routledge.

Hansen, Karen 2000 *Saluala: The World of Secondhand Clothing and Zambia*. Chicago: University of Chicago Press.

—— 2004 The world in dress: Anthropological perspectives on clothing, fashion and culture. *Annual Review of Anthropology 33*: 369–392.

—— 2005 From thrift to fashion: Materiality and aesthetics in dress practices in Zambia. In *Clothing as Material Culture*. Susanne Kuchler and Daniel Miller eds. pp. 107–120. Oxford and New York, Berg.

Harrist, Robert E. Jr. 2004 Replication and deception in calligraphy of the Six Dynasties Period. In *China Aesthetics: The Ordering of Literature, the Arts, and The Universe in the Six Dynasties*. Zong-qi Cai ed. pp. 31–59. Honolulu: University of Hawaii Press.

Harvey, P.J. and W.D. Walls 2003 Laboratory markets in counterfeit goods: Hong Kong versus Las Vagas. *Applied Economics Letters 10*(14): 883–887.

Haug, Wolfgang F. 1986 *Critique of Commodity Aesthetics: Appearance, Sexuality, and Advertising in Capitalist Society*. Minneapolis: University of Minnesota Press.

Hendry, Joy 2001 *The Orient Strikes Back*. New York: Berg.

Hermes, Joke 2007 *Re-reading Popular Culture*. Malden: Wiley-Blackwell.

Herrmann, Gretchen M. 1997 Gift or commodity: What changes hand in the U.S. garage sale. *American Ethnologist 24*(4): 910–930.

Higgins, Richard 1986 Counterfeit goods. *Journal of Law and Economics* 29(2): 211–230.

Hua, M. 2007 *Zhongguo fujuanshi.* [*Chinese Costume History.*] Tianjin: Tianjin renming meishu chuban she.

Huang Ke, and Guangyu Guo 2009 Chengdu Shanzhai Yitiaojie. [The Shangzhai Street in Chengdu.] *Chengdu Shangbao*, February 21.

Hurt, Harry 2007 Luxury, and how it became common. *New York Times*, August 19.

Intellectual Property Office Ministry of Economic Affairs of Republic of China 2005 *Annual Report 2005.* Taipei: Intellectual Property Office Ministry of Economic Affairs.

International Anti-Counterfeiting Coalition 2010 Truth About Counterfeiting. Retrieved from http://www.iacc.org/about-counterfeiting/the-truth-about-counterfeiting.php on November 18, 2010.

Jacobs, Jane 1992 *The Death and Life of American Cities.* New York: Vintage.

Jamieson, Mark 1999 The place of counterfeits in "regimes of value": An anthropological approach. *Journal of the Royal Anthropological Institute 5*: 1–11.

Jing, Jun 1996 *The Temple of Memories: History, Power, and Morality in a Chinese Village.* Stanford, California: Stanford University Press.

Jinwanbao 2010 Shanzhai chunwan youxi ma [Will Shanzhai Gala Be There?] *Jinwanbao* January 10.

Johns, Adrian 2010 *Piracy: The Intellectual Property Wars from Gutenberg to Gates.* Chicago: University of Chicago Press.

Keane, Michael A 2002 As a hundred television formats bloom, a thousand television stations contend. *Journal of Contemporary China* 11(30): 5–16.

Keesing, R. 1986 *Cultural Anthropology: A Contemporary Perspective.* Berkeley: University of California Press.

Kempen, Luuk Van 2003 Fooling the eye of the beholder: Deceptive status signaling among the poor in developing countries. *Journal of International Development* 15(2): 157–177.

Kennedy, Duncan 2010 Italian police seize counterfeits. *BBC News*, February 13.

Khan, Zorina 2002 *Intellectual Property and Economic Development: Lessons from American and European History.* Workshop paper of Commission on Intellectual Property Right.

Kooijman, Jaap 2008 *Fabricating the Absolute Fake: American Contemporary Pop Culture.* Amsterdam: Amsterdam University Press.

Lam, H. S. with W. Wong and A. Ahuja 2008 Renal screening in children after exposure to low dose melamine in Hong Kong: Cross sectional study. *BMJ 2008*(337): a2991.

Langman, C. 2008 Melamine, powdered milk and nephrolithiasis in Chinese infants. *The New England Journal of Medicine 370*(11): 1139–1141.

Laughlin Robert 2008 *The Crime of Reason.* New York: Basic Books.

Leach, James 2008 An anthropological approach to transactions involving names and marks, drawing on Melanesia. In *Trade Marks and Brands: An Interdisciplinary Critique.* Bently, Lionel, Jennifer Davis and Jan C. Ginsburg eds. pp. 319–342. Cambridge: Cambridge University Press.

Lee, Cheng-Liang 2009 *Zojingduhuizhongguo.* [*Walking into the Urban China.*] Taipei: Sino Books.

Levitt, Peggy 2001 *The Transnational Villages.* Berkeley, LA, London: University of California Press.

Li, Chun 2003 Taiwan shiyuandien huozi Yiwulai [Yiwu supplies Taiwan 10 Dollar Shop]. *United Daily Newspaper*, October 28.

Li, Shuo 2010 Chunjiejingji Shengjishindinglu. [New Principles for Upgrade Spring Festival Economy.] *Qingdao Daily*, February 23.

Li, Zhiping and Qizhi Zhang 2002 Arabian shanren duo zhongguo xiaocheng tao jin. [The Gold Digging of Arabian merchants.] *Xinhua Online*, December 2.

Liang, Bryan A. 2006 Fade to black: Importation and counterfeit drugs. *American Journal of Law and Medicine 32*: 279.

Lieberman, Marvin B. and David B. Montgomery 1988 First mover advantages: Special issue, "Strategy content research" *Strategic Management Journal 9*: 41–58.

Lien, Marianne 1997 *Marketing and Modernity: An Ethnography of Market Practice.* New York: Berg.

Lim, Louisa 2006 The end of agriculture in China. *NPR News,* May 19.

Lin, Yi-heng 2007 Woyoduoai mingpaibao? [How Much do I Love a Brand Name Bag?] *BRAND Magazine,* June 5.

Liu, J. M., Liu, Z. Z., Xu, R. Q., and Zhang, C. L. 2008 The analysis of the Report of 2007 National TV Audience Survey. *TV Research, 3(220):* 36–39.

Lu, Liang 2010 2010 Nien shenzhenrende shojiichunzheng haijianggeng yenzhong? [Will Shenzhen Citizens become More Dependent on Cell Phones in 2010?] *Southern Daily,* January 27.

Mainichi News 2007 *Character for "Fake" chosen as Kanji of the Year as food scandals rock Japan.* December 15.

Marcus, George and James Clifford 1986 *Writing Culture.* Berkeley: University of California Press.

Marx, Karl 1977 *Capital: A Critique of Political Economy,* London: Vintage Books.

Marx, K. and Frederick Engels 1986 *The German Ideology, Part One.* New York: International Publishers.

Mauss, Marcel 1990 *The Gift.* Paris: Presses Universitaires de France.

Meichtry, Stacy 2002 Special courts to put fashion fakes on trial. *International Herald Tribune,* July 25.

Meisner, Maurice 1997 *Mao's China and After: A History of the People's Republic.* New York: The Free Press.

Mertha, Andrew 2005 *The Politics of Piracy.* Ithaca: Cornell University Press.

Miller, Daniel 1994 *Modernity: An Ethnographic Approach.* New York: Berg.

—— 1995 *Acknowledging Consumption.* New York: Routledge.

—— 1997 *Capitalism: An Ethnographic Approach.* New York: Berg.

—— 1998 *A Theory of Shopping.* Ithaca, New York: Cornell University Press.

—— 2001 *The Dialectics of Shopping.* Chicago and London: The University of Chicago Press.

—— 2008 *The Comfort of Things.* Malden, MA: Polity.

Mintz, Sidney 1986 *Sweetness and Power: The Place of Sugar in Modern History.* New York: Penguin.

Minyingjingjibao 2010 Beijing Jiangguli Shanzhai wenhua fazhan [Beijing will encourage the development of Shanzhai Culture]. *Minyingjingjibao,* February 1.

Morcom, Anna 2008 Getting Heard in Tibet: Music, Media and Markets. *Consumption, Markets & Culture* 11(4): 259–285.

Morean, Brian 1996 *A Japanese Advertising Agency.* Honolulu: University of Hawaii Press.

Nagasawa, Shinya 2004 *Moet Hennessy Louis Vuitton.* Taipei: Business Weekly Publishing.

Nair, Vipin 2009 Tata motors struggles to raise cash, introduce nano by deadline. *Bloomberg,* January 11.

Nathan, John 1999 *Sony: the Private Life.* New York: Houghton Mifflin.

Nash, June 1995 Post industrialism, post-fordism and the crisis in world capitalism. In *Meanings of Work.* Fredrick C. Gamst ed. pp. 189–211. Albany: State University of New York Press.

Notar, Beth 2006a Authenticity anxiety and counterfeit confidence: Outsourcing souvenirs, changing money, and narrating value in reform-era China. *Modern China* 32(1): 64.

—— 2006b *Displacing Desire.* Honolulu: University of Hawaii Press.

Ohmae, Kenichi 2006 *The Impact of Rising Lower Middle Class Population in Japan.* Tokyo: Kodansha Publishing.

Ong, Aihwa 1999 *Flexible Citizenship: The Cultural Logic of Transnationality.* Durham and London: Duke University Press.

Padavan, Frank 2005a *The Counterfeit Connection: The Counterfeit Goods Trade, Intellectual Property Theft and Terrorist Financing.* New York State Senate Majority Task Force on Immigration.

—— 2005b *The Golden Door: Illegal Immigration, Terrorism, and the Underground Economy.* New York State Senate Majority Task Force on Immigration.

Pan, Laikwan 2008 China who makes and fakes: A semiotics of the counterfeit. *Theory, Culture & Society* 25(6): 117–140.

Paradise, Paul R. 1999 *Trademark Counterfeiting, Product Piracy and the Billion Dollar Threat to the U.S. Economy*. Westport, CT: Quorum Books.

Pellicani, Nicola 2010 Compra falsa griffe, stangata su una turista. *La Repubblica*, June 7: 19.

Penz, E. and B. Stöttinger 2005 Forget the "real" thing – take the copy! An explanatory model for the volitional purchase of counterfeit products. *Advances in Consumer Research 32*(1): 568–575.

Philip, Tim 2005 *Knockoff: the Deadly Trade in Counterfeit Goods: The True Story of the World's Fastest Growing Crime Wave*. New York: Kogan Page Publishers.

Pinney, Christopher 2002 The Indian work of art in the age of mechanical reproduction: Or, what happens when peasants "get hold" of images. In *Media Worlds: Anthropology on New Terrain*. Faye Ginsburg, ed. pp. 355–369. Berkeley: University of California Press.

Qian, Y. 2006 *Essays on the Economics of Intellectual Property Rights, Innovation and Marketing*. Ph.D. dissertation, Department of Economics, Harvard University.

Ratnapruck, Prista 2008 *Market and Monastery: Manangi Trade Diasporas in South and Southeast Asia*. Ph.D. dissertation, Department of Anthropology, Harvard University.

Richardson, Megan 2008 Traversing the cultures of trade mark: Observations on the anthropological approach of James Leach. In *Trade Marks and Brands: An Interdisciplinary Critique*. Bently, Lionel, and Jennifer Davis & Jan C. Ginsburg eds. pp. 343–358. Cambridge: Cambridge University Press.

Rivoli, Pietra 2005 *The Travel of A T-shirt in the Global Economy*. Hoboken, New Jersey: Wiley & Sons.

Rosenberger, Nancy R. 1996 Fragile resistance, signs of status: Women between state and media in Japan. In *Re-Imaging Japanese Women*. Anne Imamura ed. pp. 12–45. Berkeley, Los Angeles, London: University of California Press.

Rupp, Katherine 2003 *Gift Giving in Japan*. Stanford: Stanford University Press.

Sakamoto Koishi 2008 *Chukoku Yiwu businesu jijyo* [*Business in China's Yiwu.*] Tokyo: Doyukan.

Sassen, Saskia 1998 *Globalization and Its Discontents: Essays on the New Mobility of People and Money*. New York: The New Press.

—— 2004 *Global City*. Princeton: Princeton University Press.

Schmidle, Nicolas 2010 Inside the knockoff-tennis-shoe factory. *New York Times*, August 19.

Schwartz, Hillel 1998 *The Culture of the Copy*. Cambridge, MA: MIT Press.

Scott, James 1985 *Weapons of the Weak*. New Haven: Yale University Press.

Sennett, Richard 1992 *The Fall of Public Man*. New York: Norton.

Simmel, Georg 1978 *The Philosophy of Money*. London and New York: Routledge.

Simons, Craig 2005 Faking it. *South China Morning Post*, January 10.

Slater, Don 1997 *Consumer Culture and Modernity*. Cambridge: Polity.

Southern Daily 2009 *Shanzhai hendaichong hen minzhu*. [*Shanzhai is mass culture and democracy.*] March 4.

Stoller, Paul 2002 *Money Has No Smell: The Africanization of New York City*. Chicago, London: University of Chicago Press.

Tahara, Shinshi 2005 On the supply chain of counterfeit goods. *Nikkei BP (Japan)*, September 12.

Tam, W. and Yang, D. 2005 Food safety and the development of regulatory institutions in China. *Asian Perspective 29*(4): 5–36.

Tapscott, Don and Anthony D. Williams 2006 *Wikinomics: How Mass Collaboration Changes Everything*. New York: Portfolio.

Taussig, Michael T. 1993 *Memesis and Alterity: A Particular History of Senses*. New York: Routledge.

The Daily Telegraph 2005 *Bargain Shop to The World Feels Price-War Heat*, November 28.

Thomas, Dana 2007 *Deluxe: How Luxury Lost Its Luster*. New York: Penguin Press.

Thompson, J. W. C. 2004 *Bootleg Billions: The Impact of the Counterfeit Goods Trade on New York City*. New York: City of New York Office of the Comptroller.

Thornton, Sarah 1997 The social logic of subcultural capital. In *The Subcultural Reader*. Sarah Thornton and Ken Gelder eds. pp. 184–192. London: Routledge.

Trebay, Guy 2004 Front row: A booming black market. *New York Times*, November 30.

—— 2008 This is not a sidewalk bag. *New York Times*, April 6.

—— 2009 When Cartier was just for the likes of Liz. *New York Times,* April 26: ST8.

Tungate, Mark 2005 *Fashion Brands: Branding Style from Armani to Zara.* London: Kogan.

Ungoed-Thomas, Jon 2005 Designer fakes are "funding Al-Qaeda." *The Times,* March 20.

Watson, J. L., Ed. 1997 *Golden Arches East: McDonald's in East Asia.* Stanford: Stanford University Press.

—— 2004 Presidential address: Virtual kinship, real estate, and diaspora formation. The man lineage revisited. *The Journal of Asian Studies 63*(4): 893–910.

Warde, A. 1997 *Consumption, Food and Taste: Culinary Antinomies and Commodity Culture.* London: Sage.

Weir, Shelagh 1995 *Qat in Yemen.* London: British Museum Press.

Wood, Hannah 2009 Fake brand shopping centre set to open in China. *The Mirror,* January 5.

Wong, Winnie Won Yin n.d. The panda man and the anti-counterfeiting hero: Art, activism and the performance of appropriation. *Positions.*

Wu, Xiaodong 2010 Caogenchunwan Buneng Chengshouzhizhong [The Burden of Grass-Roots Gala]. *China News Service.* January 25.

Xie, Jingwei 2009 Anti-shanzhai law proposal sparks Row. *China Daily,* March 5.

Xin, H. and R. Stone 2008 Chinese Probe Unmasks High-Tech Adulteration with Melamine. *Science 322*: 1310–1311.

Yadley, J. and Barboza, D. 2008 Despite warnings, China's regulators failed to stop tainted milk. *New York Times,* September 27.

Yan, Xinchen 2008 Zhongguo Zhizhao dailai dierci shanzhai fengcao. [Made in China Would Bring the Second Wave of Shanzhai.] *China Southern Weekend,* August 23.

Yan, Yunxiang 2003 *Private Life Under Socialism.* Stanford, California: Stanford University Press.

Yang, Lingwen 2009 Lienfake yueh hebing yingsho 79.32 yiyuan. [MediaTek's Consolidated Income in February reached $24,787,500.] *Now News,* March 6.

Zhongguo xinwen she 2010 *Chunwan wangshi.* [*Memories of Gala.*] February 26.

INDEX